Our World in Metaphors

(Driven By the Truth)

By Eze Ihenacho

Faunteewrites Books

A division of Faunteewrites Limited

Since 2012

www.fauntee.com

Published by Faunteewrites Limited

A CIP catalogue record for this book is available from the British Library.

ISBN: 978-0-993-0417-8-5

DEDICATION

This book is dedicated to humanity, the one human race—referring to all tenants renting this one entity and globe called the world. This book has emerged in recognition of the fact that there is only one race relevant to human beings, and that is the 'Human Race.' Other races relate to dog race, horse race, and track trace. The track race, human beings can partake, and the other races are for dogs and horses.

In love and passion for humanity, I particularly dedicate this book to my late teacher parents, Prince Japheth Abanobi and Lady Christiana Nnenna Ihenacho, the entire Ihenacho Dynasty led by His Royal Majesty, Eze Dr. George Ihenacho of Isi Ogwa, Mbaitoli L.G.A, Imo State in Igbo Land. I also dedicate this book to the two countries that have had a profound impact on the person I have become (Nigeria and Great Britain respectively), and all other countries I had visited.

Finally, I dedicate this book to all the people that have crossed my path in school, church, personal relationship, work, clubs, and other public gatherings. All I am, you have contributed in making me, and I remain acutely aware that I can only be a part of the jigsaw puzzle. I would have been only too good for nothing without your additions and contributions to my life. What use would the bright eyes be if the legs refuse to move and the rest of the human body parts stop to function? Let us take a more detailed look at our world with a view to placing humanity where it ought to be. Let us appreciate and truly celebrate humanity for positive change.

CONTENTS

Acknowledgements 9

Beneficiaries 13

The Immense Power & Impact of the Truth 15

Rationale 21

Our World As An Aircraft 29

Our World As The Human Body 33

Our World As A Journey On Motorway Or Freeway 43

Our World As A Tree 47

Our World As A Football 53

Our World As A Car 61

The 'Five Finger' Theory Illustrated 65

Chicken & Egg in Humanity Resolved? 77

Inspiration! 83

How Rational Are Human Beings? 91

The 'Limited' Human Designed Academic System 97

Reasons for the malfunction in humanity 107

The Correct Order of Our World 113

Two Warring Nations over Identity 123

Generational Components to Domestic Violence 131

'Black' People & Over-Representation in Mental Health in London .. 175

Success and Failure 183

Mixed Reaction Following Receipt of Award 185

Sent to Answer A Call that Wasn't Mine 189
I Grew Up Thinking I Was a Thief.. 191
Recommendations For Posterity.. 193
Final Thoughts & Things to Consider 215
About The Author.. 217
The Author's Funeral Oration 219

ACKNOWLEDGEMENTS

It is in recognition of the fact that 'a tree cannot make a forest,' no one can prepare anything called food with one ingredient, and no matter how great anything or anyone is, that thing or individual amounts to nothing on its own. I want to express my profound gratitude first of all to Almighty God, the Creator of all things, through whom I have life and health to be who I am. I want to extend my thanks to all and sundry who have contributed to who and what I have become. I want to salute all members of Ihenacho Dynasty, people of Ogwa, Igbo community, Nigerian nation, the African continent, Great Britain, the European community and all the countries I have visited in my lifetime. In addition, I want to appreciate all the institutions I had attended—Ekwerazu Community School in Ogwa, Archdeacon Dennis Junior Seminary in Mbieri, Ahiara Technical College in Mbaise, Havering College in Romford and Middlesex University then in Enfield.

It is also in humility I want to express my gratitude to all the associations I belong to, and all formal and informal friendship (good and not so good). And an extension of my appreciation goes to my colleagues in all the Local Authorities in England where I had worked: Camden, Barking & Dagenham, Waltham Forest, Slough, Guildford, Newham, Hammersmith & Fulham, and Haringey. The experience, knowledge, and skill I possess would not have been possible without both the negative and positive things I learnt and shared with you all. Whatever I am would not have been enhanced without you. You have served as a massive engine and I as a little plug. Without you, my purpose could not and cannot be served.

Though you need me as a part of the jigsaw puzzle in order to function, I am aware that I am completely useless on my own without being plugged into you, the real 'engine.' On this note, I want to single out one of the people I came to know through Facebook, as his contribution (many may perceive as little, and he may not have realised) embodied the realities of this book. In one of my postings on 'Fb's Leading Conversation' group, I posted: *The person who needs the truth most is the person troubled by it.* However, this gentle, humane and rational man liked the post but suggested that I insert 'most' in between person and troubled.

The significance of this suggestion brought it home to me what humanity is in dire need of. I quickly inserted it, and now the quote is complete and sparked by that little plug (most): ***The person who needs the truth most is the person most troubled by it.*** When I told Bob Atkins that his contribution meant so much to me, as it captured exactly what my book was about and informed him that I wanted to acknowledge him for it, he, in his humane way, replied, "Really no need, but it's totally your call, sir." In view of this, I would like anyone using this quote to please credit it not only to me but Bob Atkins. Together, the two of us constructed the above quotation. This shows that no one is ever complete on their own and everyone is only a part of the jigsaw puzzle.

I also want to extend my appreciation to the following individuals whose inspirational work and contributions were immense to the production of this book: HRH Eze Dr. George Ihenacho of Ishi Ogwa Community, HRM Oba Dokun Thompson (The Oloni of Eti-Oni), Mr. & Mrs. Benjamin and Reine Achogbuo, Mr. Malcolm A. Benson, Dr. Alistair Soyode, Mrs. Ify Adenuga, Lady Carlyn Chidiebere Duru, Mr. Charles Joel Walker, Nassuna Ndaula, Linda Augustine, Yemisi Jenkins (MBE), Tony Fernandez, Alj. Dr. Ibrahim K. Asante, Mr. & Mrs. Emeka and Faustina Anyanwu, Jeni Plummer, Nikki Plastiras, Bob Atkins, Prince Stanley Okey Phillips, Francess Kay, Pastor Bernard & Christy Amalu (JP), Jenny Chika Okafor, Mr. Kenneth & Mrs. Oyinkansola Iwuchukwu, Dr. Cecil Eboh, Professor Rotimi Jaiyesimi, Dr. Dapo Williams, Ken Gardener, Dr. Pauline Long, Dr. Winston George Ellis, Mr. Thomas Hughes, Michaelene Gail Holder-March, Reginald Larry-Cole, Waynett Peters (Lady Million), Dr. Dayo Olomu, Vivian Timothy, Everjoy Kurangwah, Funmi Ademilua, Mr. Donatus Osuji, Professor Chris Imafidon, Pa Adebayo Oladimeji, Rev. Stanley Anyanwu (TPM) & Chief Mrs. Amoge Preety Anyanwu, Toniaamaka Chrisokere, Chief Leo & Mrs. Angela Anyanwu, Lade Olugbemi, Wilson Nwane, David Michael, Mr. & Mrs. Jameson and Joyce Simwanza, Mr. Eddie Isebor, Mr. George & Mrs. Priscilla Nwachukwu, Mrs Caroline Popoola and Dr Abbey Akinoshun.

Finally, I would always reserve my profound and special appreciation to my main mentor and a man I, like many others in Ihenacho's family, always have, and will continue, to look up to—my big cousin Professor H.N.C. Ihenacho and his brilliant wife, Mrs. Beryl Ihenacho—for their unwavering support and encouragement towards the production of this book.

BENEFICIARIES

I wish to donate 5% of the overall proceeds from the sale of this book (excluding promotional sales) to the following charities dear to my heart: Cancer Research UK, Women Aspiring Great Success (WAGS), and The Good Samaritan Foundation UK.

THE IMMENSE POWER & IMPACT OF THE TRUTH

Mr. J and his nine-year-old son

There was once a man named Mr. J who was described as 'the man with few but many words' because of his wisdom and ability to provide answers for everything. Due to his wisdom, Mr. J was consulted on a regular basis whenever there was a need to resolve difficult issues of conflict in his local community. Mr. J was a teacher who inspired many, especially his students, and amazed them with his wisdom and knowledge. He was seen as a magician who was capable of relating to anyone, irrespective of their background.

Mr. J had eight children but did not have enough money (as a poorly paid teacher) to provide for his children's needs. In order to cover up for his deficiencies and absolve himself of any blame for having too many children he could not support as he would have liked to, he resorted to blaming his inability to provide for his children on his children. Mr. J often would say to his children when upset, "If not for all of you, I would have accomplished this or that." What Mr. J did not know was that amongst his children was his fourth child who gave a great thought about anything said and done. This fourth child was a great observer of life, and through his observational and reflective ability, he began to ride a motorbike between the ages of nine to ten years; he drove a motor vehicle between the ages of 12 and 13 years.

At age 9, Mr. J's fourth child had had enough of taking the blame, feeling sad and sorry for his father's woes. As he reflected, and on many occasions, he felt sorry for contributing to his father's shortfalls in life. One day, he suddenly realised that neither he nor his sibling had anything to do with his parents' predicaments. He felt a sense of relief and frustration as he thought, No, I never wrote an invitation letter to be in this household, and as far as I am concerned, no one has told me that someone else gave birth to me and brought me here for this man and his wife to look after. Mr. J's fourth child got hold of this truth that was set to set himself and his siblings free from a baseless blame. He, however, knew he had to be cautious in his delivery. He had to wait for a perfect opportunity to deliver his new found truth which was about to dispel the confusion and manipulations of the past. He had to be careful the way he delivers this truth because Mr. J was a no-nonsense man who would not tolerate even the truth that is not delivered in a respectful manner.

When the day of reckoning came, the scene was set and the die cast. Mr. J, in his usual way, summoned his children as he always did whenever they have done something wrong, especially when something has gone missing, but no one is accepting responsibility. On the particular day of reckoning, Mr. J's fourth child laid in wait as Mr. J went through his usual motion. The reason for the summons was because an important item had gone missing in the house. Mr. J began by ensuring that all his children got the same punishment which was meant for whoever was responsible for the missing item because none of his children accepted responsibility for the missing item. Following that, he went on to his verbal admonition of his children, culminating to "I have always told you all that the situation in this house is because of you all. Your mother and I would have had a brilliant life if not for you all. We would have been able to do ... this, that, and the other, if not for all of you."

The moment Mr. J's fourth child had long waited for had come and he now carefully attracted the attention of his father by calling, in a very soft tone whilst scratching his head, "Mpam eh"—meaning "My dad oh"—and Mr. J responded in a very firm and serious tone, "Yes! What is it?" Mr. J was never in the mood to entertain any trivialities or distraction when discussing important issues. He, at all times, made his children and others aware of this. He never knew what was coming.

Mr. J's fourth child then, in a very calm, subtle, and hesitant voice and still scratching his head asked, "Npam eh, but onwekwaranu onye muru anyi kpota anyi nga?" Meaning, My Dad, did anyone give birth to us and bring us here? Mr. J was shocked on hearing this; he was so shocked he froze and, for the first time in his children's life, was visibly lost for words.

He was dumbfounded and couldn't respond. He looked at his 9-year-old child, and his wife, and everywhere was silent. Mr. J did not know how to respond to that moment of truth. He was wondering whether someone told his 9-year-old fourth child to ask such a question, as he could not believe what came out of his mouth. He did not believe the young lad could come up with such a question. He was petrified because one of his psychological weapons had been destroyed once and for all with the emergence of the truth. He did not know how to wriggle out of the 'dark hole,' as no answer could restore his grip on the psychological warfare based on unfounded reality and blackmail. He thought that was the end but did not know it was just the beginning. He never anticipated more was on its way until he decided to respond by digging another hole for himself.

Mr. J asked his 9-year-old fourth child, "Aren't you happy we gave birth to you?" His 9-year-old fourth child frowned and responded, "No! I am not happy; I was happy wherever I was before you brought me out to this miserable world. I knew no pain, no hunger, no suffering, and no sickness where I was. You should have stopped at your third child." Mr. J was shocked and did not know what to say or do. He was not only concerned with what his 9-year-old has done but was worried because his other children had become aware of the truth.

Until his death, Mr. J never used that cliché that sought to blame his children who had no contribution to their arrival for the state of his household which he and his wife designed. The truth found him out and exposed his fabrication which had served him for such a long time until his 9-year-old dismantled everything with the immense power of the truth. **This showed that the very existence of lies guarantees the preeminence of the truth.** Mr. J's 9-year-old had many tricks up his sleeves which led Mr. J to one day say to his wife, "There's something about that son of yours ... something about that boy. Hmm, only heaven knows!"

Nothing but the truth!

The truths I share with you have no duplicate and are unequivocal. They can only be subjectively, not objectively, contested. They are my little contributions to humanity, and though they are meant for every tenant of this world, only those who are in the business of deceiving themselves and/or others and those affected by delusional symptoms of mental illness will doubt, argue, or reject them from only their subjective viewpoints. The truth I give you is true because I am not a politician campaigning for votes, neither am I a preacher after 10% of anyone's income. I am only concerned about the state of humanity...the state of this one human race and this one world that is being torn apart by those renting it only for a season.

It is critical to note that no matter how big a tree is, it can only give birth to fruits in accordance with the initial seed planted. Hence no one can plant mango and expect to reap oranges naturally.

There's no need hoping for a better world or depending on any leader or anyone to bring positive change to this singular entity called the world when at the root of our existence are dangerous seeds that can only bear dangerous fruits. Seeds in the form of concepts, ideologies, and theories that are only suitable for the jungle. It is a known fact that embedded confused thought processes automatically produce confused actions.

If humanity honestly wants to see positive change in this world, then it would need to understand in details the contents of the foundation that is propelling all its activities and their dire consequences. When it does, it will seek for appropriate and conducive theories, concepts, and ideologies fit for rational human beings and relay a better and solid foundation with those. It is also of no use to think that our world would change positively by accident.

Accidents never produce anything positive; rather, they bring destruction. In order to have anything positive, one has to conceive the idea, desire the idea, plan and work persistently towards the realisation of that idea in order to bring the idea to fruition.

Only bad things can happen in an instant, and often without much thinking; war can be declared, one step only to jump into a hole, one hit to smash a car, one strike and a life is taken, but to reverse any of these, which implies positive, would require thinking, planning, time, and they must involve a process, not an event. Good and positive things have to be deliberately orchestrated in order to be achieved; they cannot be wished into existence.

At the moment in time, humanity is acting like a spoilt, lazy and hopeless brat, content to continue building with old defected blocks on top of a poorly laid foundation left by their parents. A child that is acting like a 'lunatic' expecting positive outcome whilst repeating the same old mistakes over and over again and, in the end, seeks to justify their stupidity by claiming, "We have always been this way; we are animals born to behave this way, and there is nothing we or anyone can do about it." It is my belief that every right-minded person would disagree with this position.

A clever child acts differently. A clever child would look at a defected building they inherited with a view to either making it better or building a better one from scratch, especially if the existing building is threatening their and other people's health and safety. It is a shame that this current generation, that is supposed to be (if not more intelligent than their ancestors) more exposed, has continued to subscribe to their ancestors' old and dangerous ways. These ways revolve around craft, deception, division, hatred, and wickedness, hence our world is broken. It is about time humanity woke up to reality. It is about time humanity advocated and defended this singular entity, not a part or parts of it at the expense of another or others.

Humanity, like the human body with different parts, has suffered and will continue to degenerate if human beings renting this world continue to fight and defend parts of it at the expense of other parts. What would be the state of a human body when the head is only after what it can get at the expense of the leg, or where the leg cannot do its work due to the fear of the hand? The time to start the real process of saving humanity is now.

Furthermore, one of the misconceptions and lack of understanding in humanity which contributes enormously to the malfunction we see is revealed with the saying, "I or we are better than you or them."

In a world where no two persons, even twins, are the same ... a world where no two communities or nations are same, it borders on insanity for comparatives and superlatives to be applicable (in such a world) where each person is different, unique and with special attributes meant for complementary and collaboratory purposes for the benefit of all. Can anyone imagine parts of an engine or human body behaving in this way? What will be the state of that engine and/or human body where such comparatives and superlatives are applicable?

To all those who want to be the head, not the tail, can the head be better than the neck or survive without the neck? On the other hand, will the neck survive without the head? Can the oil tell the petrol that it is better, or the radiator say to the spark plug that it is too small, it is not needed?

RATIONALE

I am an 'Automobile Engineer', and in all my life, I have not seen such a beautifully designed and awesomely made vehicle brought into my garage for repairs recently. Having not seen such a car before, I checked and found that ascribed on the front grill is 'HUMANITY.' The owner of this 'vehicle' told me that since it was purchased many, many years ago, it had always had 'Restricted Performance' warning sign on the dashboard and the original manufacturers or makers of the vehicle all died in a plane crash before they were able to look in it. The owner also told me that the vehicle had been taken to many garages, but none so far had been able to diagnose the problem. In addition, and most importantly, he said, "I met someone who recommended you, and I had no doubt that you can help to locate what the problem is. I enjoy this vehicle a lot, but sometimes I feel it would explode on me. I also wonder how wonderful it would be if the fault can be located and repaired. I would like to live and see this awesomely made vehicle perform at its best for the first time."

Having listened to all that the owner said, I agreed to investigate and put the vehicle in my specially made diagnostic equipment. I told the owner to come back the following day. The diagnostic equipment began to reveal that the makers put the inappropriate C's. Instead of putting Complement, Collaboration, and Cohesion they installed Competition, Challenge, and Contest. Thereby making different parts of the vehicle that ought to work together for the benefit of all work against themselves by wrongly thinking they are there to compete, contest, and challenge one another and each other. This, I believe, is the problem with humanity. I can't wait to break the news to the owner—because problem identified is problem solved. If the owner is happy and can understand, we can then go through the process of having the inappropriate C's removed and then install the appropriate ones. Why won't humanity malfunction when this setup means that there is division, not collaboration and unity, amongst women and men, those ascribed as black and those ascribed as white, Christians and Muslims, and amongst ethnic groups, communities, and nations?

All human beings arrive empty without preconceived ideas, without requesting to come, arrive as strangers, visitors, tenants, and must depart once their 'invincible' tenancies expire. All the things seen in this world and their various effects and implications are based on existing foundations laid before present occupants. The formation and formulation of life, attitudes, behaviours and action rest upon concepts, ideologies, and theories already established. It is unfortunate that many of these, as devised by human beings, are more suitable and relevant to animals in the jungle. Hence humanity has been and remains in crisis. The saving grace is that human beings have reflective and projective abilities which are capable of pre-empting a review with a view to devising concepts, ideologies, and theories suitable for rational human beings. If only we knew what we have missed, if only we knew what we are missing, if only we knew what we deprived ourselves, and if only can see the unharnessed and untapped glories we denied and continue to deny ourselves by holding ourselves back through holding others down, killing, oppressing, suppressing, repressing, and devaluing others. If only we knew, we would stop destroying ourselves by destroying others.

Every human being is unique, special, and important, and serves as an essential part of the jigsaw puzzle required in making the world go round. Each person carries with them unique talents and gifts that are invisible to the naked eye and difficult even for the bearer to identify. If only humanity can see what is wasted, if only the hearts of men can be opened to see beyond their noses, and if only humanity can unearth the deprivation it causes itself just by destroying an individual, community, country, or continent.

A perfect life may never be within our grasp as imperfect human beings, but as rational human beings, we can attain excellence or at the very least, we should be doing better than what we had been doing since time immemorial. Nothing good or bad is without foundation. If the world is healthy, then there will be no need to query the existing foundations. All that human being would do is to continue building on existing foundation. However, if the world is unstable, dangerous, and chaotic, then the foundations upon which every ideology is constructed would need to (at the very least) be reviewed.

In a world where the biggest threat to humanity is humanity itself, it means that all that needs to go wrong has gone wrong. All attempts now need to be made to rescue humanity from itself-designed suicidal mission. In doing so, it is critical to note that everyone conceived in the conventional way, irrespective of creed, status, stature, gender, class, ethnicity or colour, is incomplete on their own and not immune from mental illness and other afflictions of life. With this in mind, all foundations laid by human beings since time immemorial are subject to deficiencies, and each generation has a duty to not only review but implement changes that can secure the posterity of humanity. This review is critical, particularly in the areas of politics, religion, and media, in view of the immense impact these areas have on humanity.

Those born of man who were responsible for laying the foundations of operation within these three areas were not immune from mistakes and/or mental illness. Therefore, the fact that 'that's what we have always, historically done or that's the only thing or way we know' does not necessarily mean it is the right, the only, or best way to go or do things. The fact that we have been conditioned to do it that or this way does not make it right either, and the fact that it will be difficult and costly to change now does not make it impossible to change or more expensive in cost.

Whatever you do, never believe, and do not let anyone convince you that the way things are is how it was meant to be. This is not true! What we are witnessing are man-made divisions and crisis based on faulty concepts, ideologies, and theories that are at the foundation of our existence. Humanity has the capacity and ingenuity to right these wrongs. No good thing comes easy, and there is no gain without an element of pain. As much as change for good is desired, nothing will ever change for the better if business, as usual, remains the order of the day. In fact, because change is permanent, things can only progressively get worse if business, as usual, remains the mode of operation.

Humanity needs to bear in mind that in a world where the most foolish teaches the wisest how not to be stupid and leads the way in showing the wise the consequences of stupidity, no one is of no consequence, and every coin has its own value. As such, "Wisdom, knowledge, and foolishness are not commodities synonymous with any age or age group, gender, creed, status, stature, class or ethnicity" (Ihenacho 2014). The ordinary can produce the extraordinary and vice versa put in the right or wrong condition. As big as any engine is, it can take a little wire or a faulty plug to stop it from functioning. Therefore, the least amongst us is as critical as the rest of us.

Humanity needs to embrace the fact that as good as anything nature offers or it has devised, produced, or promulgated, over-reliance on any is hazardous to humanity. Some of these things are: human designed academic systems, science and technology, legislation, capitalism, religion, political correctness, bullets, and bombs. Even as good and as friendly as water is to every living thing, excessive intake of water will not give but destroy life. Hence there is something called water poisoning, intoxication, or dilutional hyponatremia. In view of this unequivocal fact, a detailed look at this book is not only necessary but pivotal, as it unravels many of the misconceptions responsible for this suicidal mission humanity has sent itself.

Our world has gone crazy because political correctness, religion, capitalism, science and technology have all gone mad. Political correctness has, within it, things like positive discrimination, zoning and quota systems, and all of these are negative to humanity. Positive discrimination simply means that "a goat can do a dog's job."

Zoning means that there is something being shared and, in turns, people can go and get their share at the expense of others. Quota means participation, representation irrespective of substance, expertise, experience, quality, and qualification. Religion means "my belief is better than yours, sowing of seeds and destruction of those without belief or different belief systems. Capitalism means here and now, fill your pocket, end justifies means, and damn the consequences. Science and technology is simply the answer or possible answer to all unanswered and unanswerable questions and mysteries. Human beings need to keep in mind that we are limited, if not by anything else, by death. Therefore, so long as we are limited, everything designed or inspired by us must be limited too, and must not be relied upon beyond its capabilities. Anything, irrespective of how useful, stretched beyond its limits will break and become hazardous to humanity. The time to do whatever it takes to save humanity is now; tomorrow may be too late!

This book does not advocate utopia, neither is it advocating for equality, because both are not only unrealistic but not right. The imperfection and limitations in human beings make actualisation of utopia an impossible proposition, whilst equality is only a colourful and plausible word that is totally not right. The world would stop when everyone becomes equal; the same way the hand would if all fingers become equal. There is nothing practical about the term 'Gender Equality,' because no two women or men are the same, let alone men and women being equal. However, the differences in each individual, gender, or colour do not make anyone more or less valuable than the other or others.

The fact that you may consume more food than me does not mean you have more energy than me, neither does it mean that you will be more or less productive than me. In fact, if there should be a priority, women should count as one and men, two, because they are the source of life, even though without men, that 'source' will not be there in the first place, let alone 'life.' This book advocates for a new way of thinking, which would help bring about the right mindset, because wrong concepts bring about wrong ideas and practices. The kind of mindset that would assist humanity in its quest to devise new concepts, ideologies, and theories suitable for 'rational' human beings.

It is critical to note that the desire for positive change will remain an illusion if we, as individuals, communities, groups and nations, continue to repeat the same old things; rather, the change we are likely to see is change for the worse, because nothing is as constant as change. This book serves as a reminder to all human beings that irrespective of who we are or become, irrespective of what group or society we belong or claim to belong to, and irrespective of how many property and businesses we own, we are all tenants to this world and must exist once our individual 'invisible' tenancies expire. Our arrival is without invitation and consent, and our departure, under 'normal' circumstances, is also without our consent.

If one thinks that it is only alcohol and illicit drugs that can intoxicate, they need to think again. It is often things human beings are not conscious of that harm them the most. Just like in boxing, the punch that knocks one out is not necessarily the most powerful but the unexpected.

Just like excessive alcohol and/or illicit drugs abuse, anything that makes one lose sight of reality in terms of how they perceive, relate to, or value themselves and/or others is not only dangerous to the individual but also dangerous to others. Let it not surprise anyone when I say that some of those things with potential to cause one to lose sight of reality and acquire the irrational feeling of superiority or inferiority (which are both dangerous to humanity) are: excessive academia/institution of learning, illiteracy, location of place of birth, material wealth and possessions, brand of uniform worn, temporary position (office) occupied in this transient life, skin colour, physical strength, and/or appearance.

Everyone needs to be mindful of these as they can turn a human being into a psychopath and/or sociopath with deadly consequences to humanity. The time to save humanity is now!

Finally, this book encourages all who have agenda for the posterity of humankind to remember that one's message has to be different in order to make the difference. Therefore, do not go for what will please the many or things that are based on the same old concepts, ideologies, and theories responsible for the awful state of affairs, for they relate to the deadly status quo. Nothing changes if everything remains the same. Do not be discouraged because many are struggling to relate to what you are bringing. When people are used to eating sweet and unhealthy things, they struggle to touch bitter and healthy things but would, in the end, be accepting them when time is up, especially when they become ill from all the unhealthy sweet things they have consumed.

Do not be discouraged, because every new idea suffers the same faith as new tricks are always challenging to old dogs. However, remain resilient, defiant, without giving in or giving up, and at the appointed time, the wheels will start to turn. Humanity is in severe danger right now, and the time to save it is now.

Just keep going and remain consistent in being objective; the few that reject you will never be able to contend with the many that accept you. Ride on!

To all those who fight and are fighting for equity and justice—be it from a feminist, civil or human rights' angle—yours are noble causes that are in tune with humanity, so long as it does not amount to forcing the oppressor into an oppressed position. This is because status quo remains the same when the oppressed swap places with the oppressor. The object is for different parts of the body to be at their best, respect each other's role, and be equally rewarded in their roles without any subduing or overlabouring the other or others.

OUR WORLD AS AN AIRCRAFT

Political correctness has plunged humanity into crisis. Concepts such as ZONING, QUOTA SYSTEM, AND POSITIVE DISCRIMINATION are very negative indeed and have threatened and continue to threaten humanity. Humanity needs to work hard and get to a level where such concepts are wiped out completely. Humanity needs to aim for quality and 'best suited' for all positions at all times, irrespective of how many times such quality is coming out from the same womb.

Every family, community, and nation is like an aircraft with passengers looking forward to getting to their individual destinations. The only thing these passengers need is a pilot to take them there. The pilot simply has to be qualified, experienced, and skilled. However, the concepts of zoning, quota system, and positive discrimination: it means that anyone can pilot the aircraft so long as they come from the particular zone of interest. It also means that a goat can do a job best suited for a dog, and an iron bar can produce water. Zoning means that leadership is nothing to do with service but all to do with sharing as people take turns to concentrate and grab the share of their particular zone whilst negating the rest. Quota means equal representation and participation based on percentages, irrespective of relevant skill, knowledge, and expertise. Therefore, it no longer matters whether one is up to the job or not; all that matters is that there is equal representation. Positive discrimination is similar to quota system as it seeks to ensure mere 'representation,' 'tokenism,' and 'participation.' Imagine an aircraft about to be piloted by someone who has no clue about the whereabouts of the cockpit! Can humanity now see one of the major reasons why it is malfunctioning in spite of its academic performance and ingenuity?

As pilots, when it comes to people in leadership positions, people are likened to 'goats doing jobs reserved for dogs' when they fail to appreciate that leadership is all about providing an enabling environment for all citizens within their particular jurisdiction to maximise their potentials.

When leaders fail to understand that the greatest and most valuable assets they have are its citizens who are the drivers of all facets of every aspect of life, they will preside over doom and gloom.

One does not need to be a rocket scientist to know that for there to be good roads, health care, and educational facilities, power supply, a judicial system, well trained and quality individuals are required. It is a crime against humanity for anyone to offer themselves or be chosen to be in a position of leadership if they are not in tune with the basic requirement which makes an investment in citizens the most important priority of any leader. No individual, community, or nation will ever fail when every individual, irrespective of ability, is enabled to maximise their unique potentials and every community harness their respective attributes and pull them together like the five fingers in order for the hand to be at its most effective.

Genuine leaders are often reluctant and only take on the role of leadership based on inspiration, compulsion, and intense desire to serve humanity, not self and/or the few. A genuine leader understands the importance of 'the small spark plug in a massive engine,' and appreciates that 'no matter how great an individual, religious group, community or nation is, they are only as good as their weakest link.'

In this malfunctioning singular 'aircraft' called the world we are all in, the effects of the malfunction affects all within it irrespective of the particular location of the fault. Each of us in this aircraft who identifies the source of the problem has a responsibility both to ourselves and others to point it out ceaselessly until something is done to remedy the situation. It is not just the responsibility of the pilot who may not be in the right frame of mind to know there is a problem. We must not say because we are also affected by it, we should keep quiet or assume that, the aircraft is built to malfunction therefore; we wait until it crashes eventually. Those who go to any length and fight to lead are often driven by self-serving interests and agendas not fit for humanity. A leader is a 'pilot' and when a pilot has no clue where the cockpit is or cannot pilot an aircraft, the aircraft and all within it will be in severe danger. **The worst thing in life is for the 'eye' to be offered, or de-**

mand to be in a position reserved for the 'leg.' A Goat will be found wanting when in a role reserved for Dogs. So is anyone without the knowledge, skill and ability in a position reserved for pilots.

OUR WORLD AS THE HUMAN BODY

Just like the human body is one with different parts for different purposes but are interlinked and connected without divisions, it is one world, one entity, and one globe without demarcations but with different individuals, communities, and nations each with unique, special, and different attributes resident within it. These differences are essential and beneficial to humanity because as important as anyone person, community, or nation is, they can only serve as a part of the jigsaw puzzle which cannot function on their own without the others.

The world was, is, and remains one but human beings decided to partition it. However, in spite of the partitioning, the sky remains unbroken, and without the use of man-made landmarks, signposts, and technological gadgets, there is no knowing when one walks from one town or one village into another. Just like the human body has different parts that are interlinked and connected without division, so our world is, until human beings began to demarcate and divide it up. In the human body, every part is well joined up; each needs the other, and anyone separated from the rest cannot survive. In the same way, no individual, community, or nation can survive or go it on their own.

Human beings inhabiting this one world (like the human body) cannot function if every individual, community, and nation becomes the same. In the same way, the body will stop to function if all its parts become the leg, for example. The differences are for different roles and purposes. No part of the body is more or less important than another, and though they are different, they are inter-linked because they cannot function as separate entities. As important as the brain is to the body, its activities will become useless if the other parts refuse to cooperate or work in partnership with it. The brain can only do the brain's job, and the brain's job is completely useless without the rest doing their part.

For the body to function at its best, each part must be healthy and strong but must work in collaboration with the rest. When one part malfunctions or stops to function, it affects the rest adversely. The adverse effect on the rest of the body parts will also be felt if any part is subdued, suppressed, or repressed by another or others. It is only natural that the body will suffer when an ailment attacks it. However, when this occurs, the body should, first of all, understand this and submit itself for medical assessment. Through this medical assessment, a prudent physician should be able to carry out tests and properly diagnose the illness which should make prognosis easier. An illness such as cancer, when diagnosed, must not be treated with Paracetamol but would need adequate treatment to deal with it—for example, Chemotherapy. It is only a bad doctor that would kill the body entirely whilst seeking to cut out a tumour. In the same way, for the world to function at its best, each individual, community, and nation needs to be strong, healthy, and independent but must work collectively in one accord with one another.

Any individual, community, or nation that is suppressed, oppressed, subdued, repressed, or malfunctions will adversely affect the rest in ways never imagined. The demise of one part will cause the rest to over-compensate, and the overall effectiveness of the world as an entity weakened. It is, however, only natural that no matter how humanity gets its various parts to function at their respective best and how efficient our world becomes, at various times, humanity and our world would experience conflicts. These conflicts may be brought about by people who are not rational or people who are affected by a mental disorder of any kind. When this occurs, the civilised and rational members of this human family would need to properly diagnose what has gone wrong, and who and what are responsible before clinically dealing with it. The intention here should be to repair the damage, but if the problem proves to be cancerous in nature, every attempt must be made to cut it out before it destroys humanity, and without destroying the entire body. It is a bad and uncivilised person that would destroy an entire village in pursuit of one bad person.

There is always a better way to a better outcome in all cases. Until humanity learns to view this world as one body and one entity which suffers when a part or parts of it suffers, humanity will continue to suffer. Humanity is being disabled because, on the one hand are nations subduing and destroying other nations, and on the other are governments of subdued nations, subduing and ruining the lives of its people. The most viable, important, and valuable assets known to man (citizens) in a world of plenty, both in size and resources, being subdued and destroyed? This is as a result of foundations built by our forbearers who were irrational in their belief that human beings are born to behave this way. I totally, unequivocally, and vehemently DISAGREE!

It is important to understand, as well as appreciate, that the word 'civilisation' has little or nothing to do with industrialisation but all to do with emotional intelligence, in terms of how human beings treat themselves and others. Is there anything civil about one who does not carry out violent act inside but does outside or one who does not destroy what they perceive as their own people but destroy people outside in the same world everyone is living? The state of our world seems to suggest that violence, for example, is not acceptable in the house but justified outside from person to person and nation to nation.

The destruction of any part of this one entity called the world is the destruction of all parts. Anyone who cannot see a bit of themselves in another person...anyone who cannot appreciate that whatever they represent to their loved ones is what another person is likely to represent to their loved ones is uncivilised and irrational, irrespective of their level of academic achievement, physical appearance, material wealth, ethnicity, or status. Any individual, community, or nation that can violate or is seen not to deal with issues relating to the human right of fellow citizens for whatever reason has no moral standing to advise others about human rights. It is one body, one entity, one world, one human family, and one human race with different parts for its good and wellbeing. Let us all work hard to defend and protect it as a whole.

In this body called the world, Africa, Asia, and women can be said to represent the hand, leg, and eye to the world, whilst Europe, America, and men represent the heart, head, and mouth of the body. As important as these parts are to the body, other parts that represent other organs, especially the one that represents the back passage, are as important and critical too because of the damage or even death they can bring to the body if they malfunction or stop to function entirely. The destabilisation of any part of the body causes the weakening and/or destruction of the body itself in the long run. It is important to note also that no matter how healthy the body is or becomes, there are cancerous genes present, which can be activated at any time. When these occur, every attempt should and must be made to cut them out in the interest of the body. At the time being, these genes seem to be present and actively destroying the body. Humanity needs to wake up and deal with them; else, they will do untold damage to this body.

The body is primarily being destroyed on three fronts, and the three fronts are as guilty as each other. The three fronts are: a) those who operate under the guise of politics but are in the psychopathic game of destabilising others and destroying lives for momentary selfish gains; b) those under the guise of religion, seeking to wipe themselves out by destroying those they perceive as outsider; and c) those in the media industry that carry propaganda, decorated lies, and malicious stories as part of agents of the destructive status quo in service to their political masters. In these three areas, as in all walks of life, good and decent people exist, but they are few and far in-between.

Humanity needs to wake up and realise that these three groups are the cancers that must be confronted and helped to change anew or be defeated. These three groups are driven by individuals with psychopathic and sociopathic tendencies. The time to wake up, understand, and stop these individuals with a view to saving humanity is now. The body, our world, would become healthy when each individual, community, and nation appreciates that each represents just a hand which can never be clean, no matter how much time is spent washing itself. A hand that can only be clean when it washes the other and the other washes it. The quest and fixation on selfish agendas and national interests is born on animalistic instincts and not compatible with rational human beings.

In this one human body, one human family and one entity, if one were to deny another their human right, they question their own humanity and sanity. Anything that brings disorganisation to any part or parts of this one body destabilises the entire structure. Therefore, the warring factions, the instigators, supporters, and suppliers of arms are all guilty.

They are all contributors to the destruction of humanity, irrespective of their language, position, location, brand of attire worn, and offices occupied. The interest of self, at the detriment of the other or others is the main cancer gripping humanity. However, the sane is acutely aware that the self is of no use and can never exist without the other.

The body will malfunction if the hand should do the job of the leg and vice versa. The beauty of humanity is denied when one with voice cannot or fails to tell their own story or has to depend on someone else or others to tell their story. We are different for our survival and posterity. Differences mean exchange and sharing. Therefore, one denies themselves and others when they cannot or fail to tell their own story.

As Dr. Pauline Long (UN Ambassador for Peace) puts it in one of the African Women gatherings held at the House of Parliament in London, "Woman, men, and children of all communities and nation need to tell their own story in their own words, their own language and they own way." She also insisted that one cannot do without the other and made it clear: "No one should invite me to anything that requires a collective effort without all concerned represented." She asked, "How can women gather and talk to themselves alone when what they are complaining about requires men's attention, consideration, and action?" It is not 'them and us' but all working together in complementary, collaboratory, and cohesive way.

Humanity needs to bear in mind that whether brown, red, white, green, or black; whether male or female and irrespective of location, human beings are unequal and different but equally human beings. It is the different that makes the difference, and without the differences, everyone and everything will become stale, useless, and unidentifiable. What will become of the body if all its parts become the leg? It cannot be overemphasised that this book is not advocating for utopia but strongly advocates that each child should have the opportunity to be the best they can be, and maximise their unique potentials for their own benefit and the benefit of humanity in general.

It will never be a perfect world. Therefore, just like weeds, evil and wrong doing will be inevitable in this world we are all renting as tenants. Same as in a perfect body; illness will always attack at one point or another. However, evil worsens when the farmer, whose duty it is to rid the farm of weeds in order to give the planted crops a better chance to do well at harvest time, begins to plant the weeds themselves in addition to those that grow naturally. The leaders of this world have contributed in sowing seeds of discord that are damaging humanity.

This is the summary of what is going on. Hence a broken world is the by-product. Extraordinary people have done ordinary and wicked things that placed citizens of this world in danger; it is now time to find ordinary people who can do the extraordinary to bring sanity to humanity.

Humanity needs to accord respect and honour wherever it is due, and based on the most humble and noble, not arrogant and stupid. However, human beings need to learn to demystify limited human beings for the progression of humanity. It is a fact that the body can soldier on but not function effectively without certain parts of the body—for example, the legs—but will not survive without the head. However, as useful as the head may be to the body, its usefulness can only be relevant when linked to the body, as it becomes useless and dies once detached from the body. No one renting this world as a tenant is untouchable, because all will be touched by death, whether they like it or not.

Remember, it is only human to plan for the future; however, do ensure you live in the 'here and now,' not in the future, because the future does not really belong to anyone. Anyone who cannot offer their penny now will not offer their pounds later. Therefore, each hand, no matter how big or small, cannot get the two hands or itself clean on their own. It must take the two giving their very best—by washing each other—for both hands to be clean. As such, all the parts of the body...every aspect of humanity needs to be enabled to give all within its capacity to make the body our world, a healthy and safer place for all its tenants. The body will malfunction if the hand offers itself or is chosen to do the job of the neck. **As an individual, community, and nation, the idea of 'ruling a world' came in as a stranger—psychopathic and sociopathic; the issue is, who can be the sane brain to recognise the uniqueness and importance of each part and organises each part in such a way that**

they play their respective, peculiar, and special role in order the make the world a healthy and safer place to live?

Let's develop the insight to know that humanity is one—like a human body with different parts for different purposes for the posterity and benefit of all. Some parts are big, some small, some strong, and others weak. However, the size and strength of each part does not mean they are more or less important than another or the rest, because none, irrespective of how big and powerful, can survive on their own.

The strengths the strong ones possess are for the benefit of all, not for intimidating or attacking the weaker others. The hands are strong, but they are there to ensure that the body is well nourished and looked after. They are not there to undervalue, intimidate or beat up the legs, head, or any other part of the body. The teeth being the strongest are there to ensure that nothing solid passes through the body without being checked and, if need be, crushed to prevent harm. The teeth do not use its strength to intimidate members of the same body, for if the fingers become afraid of the teeth, how would they feel comfortable in bringing food to the mouth?

It is obvious that the body would persistently malfunction if the hands begin to threaten the legs or seek to damage it. The body will also malfunction if the leg is afraid of the hand and loses its independence and ability to give its service to the body. It would also be futile for the body if, in fear, all the leg does is to ignore its role in preference to that of the hands.

Disaster awaits the body if the teeth begin to threaten to bite off the fingers if they do not supply exactly what they demand or dictate what the fingers do. The body can only be healthy when each part is strong, healthy, and independent to harness its peculiar and critical attributes in service to itself and in collaboration with the rest in service to the body. Though where there's weakness in any part of the body, other parts should assist, none is there to make another redundant or weaken its potentials. The fear all parts should have is for ailments that come to attack the body, and they all have a collective responsibility to fight against any ailment that comes to attack the body. The parts are not there to fear but to respect one another in their respective and unique roles.

In view of this, the physical strength of any community or nation and weakness of another is there for the benefit of all, not intimidation, over-valuing, or undervaluing of any part.

Humanity is at odds with those who feel they are useless and, upon this feeling, fail to contribute the quota which only they can best contribute to humanity. On the same token, humanity frowns at those who feel more important than others and, upon this feeling, fail to realise their shortcomings and suppress others from contributing their quota. Humanity is opposed to these and blames them for the malfunction and crisis in this world we are all renting as tenants, only for a season.

We are Gods only collectively, as none of us can be God on our own. We are Gods because we are the only species on earth made by the hand of God, with the breath of God and free will to even disobey God, if we choose. Our disobedience does not prevent or stop us from being Gods once we can work collectively in a complementary fashion. It is the act of different parts bringing their respective attributes and working together with a common purpose that activates the God in us because, no matter how clever, no human being on their own can recreate or reinvent on their own. Those who are divisive and work as separate individual entities achieve little or nothing compared to those who work together as a team.

Humanity is in tune with all those who are aware of their particular strengths but, at the same time, recognize their shortcomings. Those who appreciate that they can only serve as parts of the jigsaw puzzle that are useless on their own, but effective and efficient when working in a complementary fashion to bring out the best in one another in service to humanity.

Humanity is fed up and tired of the 'peaceful,' 'inactive,' and 'silent' majority who stood by and watched evil like the Holocaust take place. The same majority are standing by today whilst the minority determined to destroy humanity, including themselves, are on the rampage! Humanity needs to wake up to the fact that those who fail

to not only learn the lessons but also fail to put mechanisms in place to prevent evil history have voted for evil history to repeat itself with devastating consequences. Humanity also needs to know that the 'peaceful,' 'inactive' and 'silent' majority are at best as bad, and at worst, worse than the minority wreaking havoc on humanity.

OUR WORLD AS A JOURNEY ON MOTORWAY OR FREEWAY

Nothing can best describe human lives and living in this one entity called the world, best like travelling on a motorway, highway or freeway—whichever takes one's fancy. Many things about our journey on this broad road are replicated in the life we live, except the fact that our entry into a motorway is mainly by choice, but our entry into this world has nothing to do with any of us. No one born of 'man' has a clue about the nation or womb that would bore them. However, once on a motorway, irrespective of the point of entry, one would notice that they are not on their own, no matter the situation they found themselves. They are likely not to be the first nor the last on the motorway. Those within one's vicinity represent those in similar circumstances, those in front represent those in better-off situation, whilst those behind are people in worse-off situation. The motorway offers each user a guarantee of 'no condition is permanent,' as any vehicle can be overtaken and can overtake also. No condition is permanent—meaning that so long as one remains alive, their condition is subject to change.

The human condition on the broad motorway is such that no matter how bad one's condition is, there will be others in similar or worse situations. It is all to do with the attitude one adopts in dealing with their situation. Each vehicle represents a visitor and a tenant renting the motorway for only a period. Therefore, each must have an exit ahead of them, as none will remain on the motorway indefinitely. Any vehicle that deludes itself to think that it owns the motorway or would remain on the motorway forever is either psychotic or psychopathic. One would also notice that there is all manner of vehicles—different makes, models, engine and body sizes—heading towards different directions, with different purposes and differing contents.

Though there are different and similar vehicles, they are all equally vehicles. Their different sizes and looks have nothing to do with their contents or performance. Their differences do not give them different rights on the motorway; rather, they all have equal rights. Irrespective of their differences, there is no way of one knowing the full value or worth of any vehicle's contents, irrespective of their position on the motorway, by mere looking at them.

The contents of a small mini car could hold more value than a big truck, but both the mini and truck drivers are not to know that. In fact, the content of the little mini car could be what the truck driver and many others are desperately in need of. The content/s could be linked to the survival and posterity of the truck driver and humanity in general, but the truck driver is not to know that through what their eyes can see from the outside. Irrespective of the importance of the contents of the mini to the truck driver, in particular, every vehicle has a unique and specific mission which, in the grand scheme of things, represents a part of the jigsaw puzzle.

Now, imagine a situation where the truck decides to knock off and destroy the mini car based solely on what it can see or for whatever reason. Imagine a situation where the truck decides to block off and halt the advancement of the mini or feels that subduing, repressing, and suppressing the mini would benefit it. Imagine a situation where survival of the fittest becomes the mode of operation on the motorway. The number of accidents and destruction of oneself through the destruction of the other and others will be incalculable. The momentary 'gains' will be nothing compared to the long-term loss and devastation as a result of the application of concepts such as dominance, superiority, and inferiority to unequal but equally important vehicles with peculiar attributes meant for the benefits of all.

As a result, irrespective of how important each vehicle and their mission is, none is more or less important than another or the others because of the uniqueness of each—in terms of contents. Every vehicle has as much right as any other to be on the motorway as long as it fulfilled all requirements. Where the requirements are not met, there has to be a formal agreed, fair-for-all process to deal with that, irrespective of the content/s or vehicle involved. Though the truck may consume more fuel and take up more space on the road, it still does not make its purpose more or less important than that of the mini. The only slight difference between what goes on in real life and what happens on the motorway (as indicated above) is that in real life, no one contributed in any way, shape, or form to their arrival on this earth, but on the motorway, people often make the choice to go on it. However, once on it, it is a matter of time before everyone reaches their respective exit as no one will remain on it. It is only an insane vehicle that claims ownership of the motorway and accuses another or other vehicles of not having the right to be on it and seeks a means of getting rid of or interrupting such vehicle/s. Each vehicle has a particular exit and only in an accident will there be more than one exit at the same time.

Sadly, this is our world and humanity in a nutshell. Superiority, inferiority, and dominance as linked to unequal but equally important human beings are inventions of psychopaths and sociopaths who did and still do not know what respect, let alone, mutual respect means. Individuals with no clue what the little plug represent in a massive engine and the immense impact of the absence of petrol in a vehicle that requires it to function.

It is a no-brainer to suggest that a car which has always malfunctioned due to the installation of the wrong parts is designed naturally to malfunction when it is obvious that all it requires is the genuine parts for it to be in perfect condition to give maximum and reliable service. The above metaphoric statement applies to humanity and this singular entity called the world we are all renting as tenants. It is not natural for humanity to malfunction the way it is today. The state of our world is an indication that humanity had been, and continues to be, propelled by the wrong concepts, ideologies, and theories upon which the foundations of our world were laid.

The best way to appreciate the similarities and equality of humankind, even though human beings are unequal in size and have different attributes, is the sky view of a motorway. No one can pick out the background, colour, creed, gender or ethnicity of the driver of any vehicle from the sky.

Being big or small is a fact and necessity of life, but feeling big or small is not necessary and wrong. Differences are critical for the existence, survival, and posterity of humanity in this one world all are renting as tenants. Humanity would not function if one size fitted all. However, being physically bigger, smaller, shorter, or taller does not make anyone more or less important than another or others, because each is different and unique for a purpose. After all, out of every Goliath, there's a David. Failure to understand this is a deformity of the mind that requires attention and cure. Therefore, stop fighting for equality; fight for justice and respect for unequal but equally important human beings. No two persons are equal, and each has their respective and valuable values.

OUR WORLD AS A TREE

The tree has the whole mark of humanity as one entity with different parts. For it to be a tree, it must begin with a seed or stem, have root, trunk, stem, branches, and leaves. Without the seed, there will be no root; without the root gathering water and nutrients from inside the ground, there will be no trunk; without the trunk, there will be no branches; without the branches, there will be no stems and no leaves; without the leaves, the tree will not have the sugar and starches it requires, which the leaves bring from the sunlight through the process called photosynthesis. As important as the root, the root cannot answer, survive, or bear fruit on its own without the other parts. Every part is different and with a different role to play for the tree to be fully functional and productive.

No part of the tree is more important or should ever be bigger than the tree itself. Though they are different with differing roles, none is more or less important than the other or others, as each needs the role of others to survive. There will be no tree if all the parts stop being different and become one. Any unhealthy part of the tree affects the overall potency and production of the tree. The root cannot do the job of the leaf, and the leaf cannot do the job of the stem. For a tree to be healthy, its various parts have to be healthy, strong, interlinked and connected with one another and each other. Any part that is not linked to the tree, cuts off, or separates itself from the tree cannot survive, no matter how big it is or the level of importance it attaches to itself. Any tree whose branches are cut off from the tree cannot bear fruits; the branches detached from the tree will be deprived of water and nutrients coming from the root and will surely die. Any tree without a root cannot remain standing.

Humanity is captured right here (spiritually and temporally). There has to be a mixture of similarities (the baseline or the root) holding the vital differences that make the entire thing functional. Human being needs to choose 'similarity' or 'baseline,' instead of equality, and anything after that is referred to as differences. The root forms that central point and the common denominating factor, just like the base that holds all the fingers together. This confirms, in religious terms, for example, that there are different pathways to the central root (God). It simply could not be one way only. Though Jesus Christ said, "I am the way, the truth and the life," but He never said, "I am the only way." The various branches, just like various routes leading to a particular destination. What will be the state of the tree if each branch starts fighting the other, forcing the rest to be like it, or killing off the rest for not being like it?

In life, there are many trees for different purposes and reasons. Can anyone imagine a world where only one tree exists, a particular tree wants other trees to become like it or deprives other trees the food they need in order to survive and bear their particular fruits? Where would the bananas, kiwis, apples, and oranges come from if all trees were mango trees? Every individual, family, community, and nation is built like a tree with different parts that play different roles but are linked and connected seamlessly.

The seeds sown and the ground upon which they are sown determine what happens to the root and productivity of the tree. This is the same with every Child. Every child routes from a family of sort, and the family is at the root of every child. Any child that separates themselves from their family loses its source, and though they may live on, the real ingredient that makes them whole will be missing, and their real happiness denied, unless their root (family) is rotten. Any family as a tree that is disjointed runs the risk of not producing good fruits or fruits at all.

The loss of a branch will reduce the number of fruits a tree produces, but the loss of the root will condemn the entire tree. This means that no matter how academically educated and/or materially rich a child becomes, they will never feel or be complete when disconnected from their family.

The impact and consequences of the root

No tree can stand firmly without a root or bear good fruits if the root is rotten or unhealthy. No parent will treat another parent's child anyhow if they know that the child's family (the root) has ways and/or means to make life difficult for them. The lack of respect and/or maltreatment individuals suffer in 'foreign' countries are often to do with what is going on in those individuals' countries, which represent the root.

Any country that is well organised with strong economic and political base that values its citizens guarantees the health and safety of its citizens worldwide. Is it not obvious that the failure of Africa to harness its true potential and take its rightful place in the world is the biggest threat to its citizens worldwide? Is it possible that many 'black' people will be murdered in America, for instance, if their real base or root Africa and the Caribbean are strong? Without economic and political strength which all nations and continent should have, these inhumane acts will continue to happen and continue to threaten humanity. Resorting to a marching club that marches each time there is a murder may gain some media coverage but yields nothing in real terms. The roots of most other communities are stronger—for example, Asia, Jewish, Chinese—hence, no one attempts to carry out such scale of inhumane acts against their citizens.

Is it not better to save many by sacrificing one than lose many in trying to cover up, pretend, or keep silent? Are we not better off to 'hands up' and accept that it takes two to tango, lay ourselves bare, identify our individual and collective errors, and even if they are not to benefit or save us, review them with a view to making things better in order to point our children and future generations to the right direction so they would be less likely to fall victim to the same trap that engulfed us? Or are we content to hand over to our children the dangerous baton that has wrecked our lives to repeat or even make worse mistakes?

At the root of every child's behaviour is primarily the dynamics of their family. At the root of every family is the dynamics of the culture and tradition of the particular community in which that family is located. When the tradition and culture of a community is such that strengthens families and enables every child within it to be the best they can be, children turn out better. A structured child is a nurtured child. A life that is not orderly is a disordered life.

The norms of every family needs to be established prior to the arrival of any baby. As much as differences are critical, there has to be a common norm that defines all cultures, traditions, and creeds. At the base of our differences should be respect for human life and differences, and understanding that whatever you represent to your people or your people represent to you is what I am likely to represent to my people, and my people represent to me. Nothing confuses a child more than when an adult is saying one thing and doing another in the presence of the child, or one parent is saying one thing, and the other parent is doing another. Once the root is rotten, the tree malfunctions.

It's mysterious and metaphoric, but it is unequivocally true. As leaves and fruits sit at the very top of trees and plants, so are leaders on this planet earth. Both are up there to provide vital services not only to trees and plants but humanity also. However, they are heavily supported by the roots, trunks, stems, and branches. They complement one another because of their differences and different roles. They are not in competition, and none is there to show superiority or feel inferior to the other. None is there to subdue or devalue another. None is there to be fearful or intimidate another or others, because each part is critical to what happens to the trees and plants in terms of survival and productivity.

The leaves provide enormous service to trees and plants by converting sunlight into energy through a process called photosynthesis. The leaves and fruits also act as manure when they fall off and die, whilst the fruits are there to feed the many. Being at the top simply means giving service, and nothing else!

In view of above, any leader who does not understand and give service to their citizens is a psychopath, sociopath and a fraud.

The various parts and individuals that make up this one human family are interrelated and interconnected just like a tree. If all the parts of the tree were to be the root, for example, it will no longer be a tree and will not be fruitful. If a tree loses one branch, its producing ability will reduce, because no branch can give more fruits that it is capable of producing, and none can replace the one lost. The same will be the case if any of the branches is suppressed or becomes useless. Humanity needs to grasp this reality fast, adjust its thought process, and revive itself.

Finally, use what you are given or obtained to serve, not oppress yourself by oppressing humanity. Like me, you are only a visitor and a tenant to this world we are all renting, with particular goods to deliver and depart. Have you visited the hospital, crematorium, and graveyard lately? If you have not, please do, because, whether we like it or not, each of us will someday visit and/or retire to one of these destinations for good. This is because no matter who or what we think of ourselves, no human being, indeed, no tenant of this world can control illnesses and/or death. The quest for finding answers to death through 'limited' man made science may be a possibility. But, the challenge to put a body burnt into ashes through fire would prove difficult to achieve and, if science becomes able to restore life to a deceased body, how would it restore life lost through ghastly accidents?

We are all 'trees' and, like different trees, we are planted—each with their peculiar and unique name, size, value, and taste. Let no tree fight to make all trees the same; where would we get our oranges from if all trees become mango trees?

OUR WORLD AS A FOOTBALL

Our world is round like a football, and in the game of football, there are different players for different positions. The players will never be equal in size, skill-set, and will have different pay scales, but they are all equally players and none is more or less important than another or others. It is ironic that everyone around the world recognises football. If one were to take a vote on the most admired, most entertaining, and the most watched team sport around the world, the 'beautiful game' of football would win easily. If one throws a football up or anything with a round shape to a crawling baby, the baby would likely give the football a chase in order to play with it. If one throws a football at a crowd, it is likely that someone would want to kick it or play with it. Everybody, including those who do not want to take part in it, can relate to football.

In the game of football, players do not choose which part of the football they catch, kick, or play with. There are huge lessons coming from the shape of football, players, and teams, in relation to human beings' social interactions and the world they live in. At a glance at the rounded shape of football, one would notice that there are usually demarcating lines. However, these lines are interlinked, seamless, and must be knitted together in order to form the round shape. It can never be a proper football if any part of it is damaged or not properly connected with the rest. If it suffers a puncture in any part of it, it affects the rest and the football may still be kicked about but would lose its bounce and will not be as effective.

Is it not amazing that football is a language that transcends culture, traditions, and nationality? A language every corner and part of the world understands. Take a football to any part of the world; one may not be able to communicate with another person in their local dialect but would find many people to kick a football around with. If one assembles eleven players from different parts of the globe with different languages, even without a coach, they would play together against another team and know when a goal has been scored. The football would serve as the common denominating factor. Could this be because of the fact that football has the same shape as the world that makes it a language for all nations?

Football is a team game; therefore, no individual would be able to play on their own whilst playing in a team. The individuals within a team would have to work together, with each position playing its part for a goal to be scored. Even though one can help out a teammate, no player can play in two positions at a time. Each position has a specific and unique role to play in order to secure the team's objectives, which is always to win. When a goal is scored, the celebration is not restricted to the scorer but the entire team. The player who scored, if humble, would recognise that without the effort of the team, they would not have been able to score. It is rare that a player picks up the ball and scores on their own, without the contribution of another player.

Yes, a player may receive a pass from the kick-off and proceed to score a wonder goal through solo effort, but the player couldn't have done that without receiving the pass from kick-off. The only way a player would be known to score on their own is if, following the kick-off whistle, a player hits the ball straight from kick off without passing to anyone and scores. These are very rare events and almost impossible in top flight football because, first of all, the player would not be able to generate the power required (whilst standing next to the ball) to beat a talented goalkeeper from the centre of the pitch, which is at least fifty yards from the opposition's goal post. Even if the player takes a run up to the ball, the goalkeeper would be able to adjust themselves to prevent the goal because of the travelling distance.

Since no one can score from the kick-off, any other form of goal is likely to be scored through the team effort, even when a goalkeeper hits a wonder shot that beats the opposing goalkeeper. This is because the ball could not have reached that keeper without the contribution of one of his or her teammates on the pitch—because, by rule, goalkeepers do not take part in kick-offs. Therefore, it is important to stress that no matter how good a striker is, if the goalkeeper concedes more than the striker scores in any particular game, the striker can only celebrate his or her goal/s but would not be able to celebrate a win. Hence, it is said that one is as good as their weakest link. Also, no matter how great a striker is, he or she has to represent only an important part of the jigsaw puzzle, which becomes useless on their own without other players participation.

The best teams are not teams with brilliant individual players who play for themselves, but teams with good individual players playing together, working hard and covering for each other as a team. In teams where a particular position is weak, other people playing in that team over-compensate and the overall output of such team is likely to reduce. In strong teams, everyone understands their role, is efficient and effective in their role, respects other teammates' roles, covers for one another, and brings together their collective effort in one accord for the benefit of the team. In football, individual players at one time or another, for one reason or another, may begin to feel they are more important than the team or even the club they play for. This is usually borne out of ignorance, short-sightedness, and a lack of insight.

No one can be a great player on their own. But if a player thinks they can be great on their own or more important than the team, such player should move on or be included at the peril of the club, as they are certain to destroy team spirit. No single player can be bigger or more important than the team, no single player can be called a team, and no single player can represent or play as a team. No matter how important a player or group of players are, the overall interest of the team would be more important and central to decision making. In the same way, no individual, family, community, or nation can claim to be more important than the world they are only a part of or claim to rule the world.

In this world, humanity belongs to one team with different individuals, communities, and nations in different locations for different purposes. Just like in football where the success and failure are not individually based but team based, the success and failure in our world is not individually but collectively based. No disorganised team, no team that fights amongst itself, and no team with factions within it can succeed. The same applies to our football-like rounded world; everyone, through their actions or inactions, contributes to the status quo. Our world is the way it is because of factions, conflicts, wars, discords, and infighting.

The pressure pot humanity has found itself in today is a build up from a culture of delusion that one can survive by destroying another or others in the same world we are all sharing. This culture meant that people, as individuals, communities, and nations, have set out deliberately destroying and rendering others useless. Hence people who ought to have stayed where they were are having to run away from destruction and converging on where they perceive as peaceful. However, as they converge, another layer of crisis is born, which can never be sustainable. So long as there is air which is not man-made, any pollution in any area, no matter how far it is, must spread and its destination cannot be controlled by man.

In this world, human beings, as individuals, communities, and nations, irrespective of everything, are like siblings. The fact that one is older or got an idea about something first does not mean they are more talented than their younger ones. It does not mean they should cheat, steal, intimidate, subdue, or suppress their younger ones either. It does not also mean also that the older is superior or should condemn their younger ones subservient to them. The older rather has a duty to ensure the young ones are protected and assist them reach their full potentials in order to have a strong, efficient, and effective family. The younger should also ensure that they do not limit or relegate themselves to what they are not or allow themselves to feel inferior due to age or size. Both young and old have a duty to work in a complementary fashion to achieve their respective potentials.

Our football-like and round world was here before each of us met it and it would remain as we each wave goodbye to it. Each of us arrives as a part of a jigsaw puzzle that is only useful when we complement the other and others. None of us will play another person's part, as no two persons are same. Though we are all human beings, I cannot be you, and you cannot be me. This is one of the lessons of the 'Five Finger' theory.

Each of us as members of a football team is special, unique and different, but none is more or less important than the other or others. Every player in all the positions is critical to the performance and achievement of the team and none should be over or under valued because, the team is as good as its weakest link. All that's needed is respect for self and others. It can only be abnormal for any individual, community or nation to misunderstand this and/or think differently. Such abnormality can only be a byproduct of irrational thought process which stems from psychological deformity. Such abnormality requires urgent attention for the posterity of humanity. If hearing aids and guide dogs can be deployed for those who are hard of hearing and poor eyesight; there is hope for those with such psychological deformity.

In this field of play called the world, each of us as an individual, religious group, community or nation as players will make mistakes. The hope is that, the mistakes we make are not the 'goalkeepers mistakes' which often are irreversible. It is hoped also that, when such mistakes occur, there are team mates to remedy the situation so the effects are not too costly for us and humanity.

If our world were a football team currently, the manager will not only be sacked but will be imprisoned.

Pride and/or fear will destroy humanity, but bravery action and humility can save it.

Humanity needs to learn that the fact one introduced or invented something does not mean that they will remain the best at that thing. One may invent, the other could advance on the inventions, and others may perfect the invention. Just like in football, those that invented it are not the best at playing it today. For that sake, the following are noted below:

Woe unto that parent who deludes themselves to think that their child would never develop their own minds or becomes so wicked to subdue, repress, and suppress their child in order to leave the child dependent on them forever. Such are parents without vision and agenda for growth and without the knowledge that even their children are individuals with unique attributes for their parents' benefits even as they grow old, let alone in their old age. Woe also unto those parents who are resistant to learning from their own children only on the premise of parenthood and irrespective of the numerous experiences their children have had, which they (the parents) do not have. Those parents who stupidly are too proud but unable to distinguish the wood from the tree.

A child needs to grow and develop their own mind ... to avoid being forever reliant on their parent, even in adulthood, and gripped with fear, even in the knowledge of the truth. Woe unto that adult child who cannot see the mistakes of their parents but just agree with everything in the belief that subscribing to their parent's lies and bad behaviour means obedience and respect to their parent. Woe to that adult child who has no understanding that the truth is no respecter of a person and never disrespects anyone. In a rounded world, one only needs to get one person (one part) wrong, and the rest is affected adversely. This is because every person, every community, and every nation is uniquely different and irreplaceable.

Half-baked is as bad as unbaked cake. They are both dangerous. As such, humanity is dangerous for being either half- or unbaked. A huge chunk of our animalistic, instinctive behaviours is retained when we have not gone through the three stages of nurturing needed for us to become rational. One who has presided over a chaos cannot claim or assume to be rational or wise. The shameful state of humanity and our world are indicative of our confused and ill-informed state of mind which human beings try to mask with limited human designed academic intelligence, science & technology, material wealth, fashion, status, awards, and titles. Well, amidst all these trivialities, we should and must find time to go back to the drawing board. We need to develop a proper insight lest we self-destruct beyond repairs.

Is it shameful and cruel for anyone who claims to be righteous, wise, educated, rational, and in charge to ask why someone is running to safety when they (the wise) contributed in setting the victim's house on fire? Is it rocket science to know that when one punctures any part of a world designed as football, every part of the world will adversely be affected in a way, shape, or form, be it immediately or in the long-run? Though a deflected football can still be kicked about, it will not be fit for its genuine purpose. Humanity at war with itself!

Humanity is like medication; very potent when it comes to curing and subduing symptoms of illnesses when used appropriately. However, it can become futile when labelled and/or used wrongly for the wrong illness or wrong dose. If humanity fails to go through the three stages of nurturing required in order to become rational, it will continue to malfunction, and no one will be safe. The truth may be uncomfortable, but it remains that bitter pill responsible for our recovery but difficult to swallow. Humanity needs to embrace the truth and stop being in denial, fearful, stubborn, or foolishly proud, so that the immense job of reconstructing this world for the posterity of humanity can commence.

OUR WORLD AS A CAR

A car is one singular entity with different parts. There will be nothing called a car if it is made of only one part or all its parts become one. Each part has a specific and different role to play and contributes to the rest for the car to function. A car functions at its optimum when all its parts are healthy and fully functional. It will be weird for the tyre or steering to seek to make all other parts become like them. It is weird because if, in the end, they achieve that by force, both will no longer recognise themselves and, of course, the car will cease to function.

Most importantly, it is crucial to note that as big as any engine, it can take something as little as the malfunction of a wire or plug to grind the engine to a halt. It is also the case that any car or engine that is built to operate on patrol will cease to function, no matter how good it is, in the absence of patrol. This simply highlights the importance and value of the least amongst humanity. Every currency has its value, and none is without consequence. The little one you are seeking to eliminate, damage, or convert to be like you could hold the key to your very existence through the little difference it has, but you are not to know that. Once again, humanity needs to learn that it is made different for its own good. The different makes all the difference.

A clever and wise child will not continue to build on dodgy foundation left by their parents and papering over cracked walls; rather, they will review the foundation with a view to relaying a solid foundation for health and safety purposes.

There are horses, and there are courses; there's always a reason why something is either good or bad. There's no way our world will function properly when all the pillars designed by men holding it are dodgy, faulty and false. Are we expecting an iron bar to produce water? Any vehicle designed to run on diesel will malfunction and eventually grind to a halt if it's filled with unleaded petrol. Humanity is designed to run on truth through the fulfilment of the three stages of nurturing, but it has malfunctioned; it will continue to malfunction and eventually destroy itself because it has been run on falsehood through limited and inadequate nurturing which could not eliminate its animalistic instincts.

It is impossible for anyone who had taken part or is currently taking part in both the maintenance of the structures and leadership of this world to claim or be ascribed as wise unless it is driven by a total lack of insight. Looking at such a broken world where, consequently, as a result of the foundations laid from time immemorial, humanity has reached a level where children are stabbing follow children to death, some women in parts of our world in 2016 are still using leaves for sanitary towels, law enforcers administering capital punishment on the streets and wars, conflicts, and disorder raging everywhere one cares to look, it is clear that the managers of this world have no clue and remain in denial. It is also clear that this generation is unwise as we have carried on building on old and faulty foundations whilst justifying our woes by either claiming 'we are designed to be the way we are, so we can't do anything about it,' or pretending that everything is okay when children are stabbing children and humanity is waging war on itself.

The time to do whatever it takes to save this one entity called the world and humanity is now. Continuing with the ideology that seeks to take care of one or two parts of the world at the expense of another or others is, and will remain, futile to humanity. Is it possible that the human body will be healthy and/or survive if the brain seeks to damage the hand or restrict the hand for momentary 'gains'? Only the inly blind will struggle to see and understand this. We have a perfect opportunity, as a generation, right now to begin the process of laying a solid foundation based on the truth for the posterity of humankind. Let's go to work bearing in mind that any reference in this book to a 'massive engine' refers to our world, and the impact of a small 'plug' refers to the tiniest part of our world.

The Truth

The truth is not interested in what people want to hear, say, or do. It does not give a damn about people's preferences, assumptions, and emotional feelings. It is also not a participant in a popularity contest. The truth is only interested in being the truth that dispels the lies, irrespective of who the liar is or purports to be. Embrace it for your own good and let's save humanity with it together.

If it is objectively contestable, it cannot be the truth. The truth can only be subjectively and equivocally contested, hence 'Whose truth?' The truth is objectively irrefutable, unequivocal, unshakable, and irresistible. It is only the truth that can save and set humanity free, nothing else. Lies, deceit, or being in denial have ruined and will continue to ruin humanity, and no bubble is safe out there.

Only the confused academically educated and/or illiterate who seeks to confuse others can ask, 'Whose truth?' for the truth lives on! The truth can only be contestable, challenged and equivocal from a psychopathic and/or psychotic perspective. On a psychopathic level are those manipulative agents who deliberately use everything within their grasp to confuse and convince others that brown is black for their selfish ends. These are the dangerous people destroying humanity and the world. On the psychotic level are those who, through a chemical imbalance in their brain, genuinely believe, as a result of illness, that brown is black. These are people are in need of help and are more of a danger to themselves than anyone else. They are treatable and get better with treatment and support.

As higher beings, our existence is linked to nature, but our survival is linked to nurturing. Nature favours other animals, but if human beings depend on nature, it will not survive. Most other creatures establish independence very quickly. A normal puppy will walk within minutes and independently find where to feed. Even our fellow primates establish independence within three years. No one born of a woman will walk within four months, let alone find where to feed. We may be the only species on the planet to know that every creature survives by feeding on other creatures, but white, brown, and black horses do not kill and eat themselves. Lions may fight for other reasons but unlikely to kill one another for their feeding; rather, they work together in partnership to ensure their feeding.

Humanity should have no problem with any individual, community, or nation. However, it should have a real problem with individuals, religious groups, communities, and nations who devalue themselves or feel superior to others and want to force others to become like them or want to become exactly like others. Such are the scums of this earth driven by psychopathic tendencies. They are devoid of the basic understanding that 'as big as any engine, it can take something as little as the malfunction of a wire to grind it to a halt.'

All the crisis confronting humanity, from bad leadership to terrorism, stem from individuals, groups, communities, and nations in this bizarre mode. They are the cancers destroying and seeking to destroy humanity. Every cancer needs to know, however, that if it succeeds in destroying a human being, it must die as well. Humanity has a duty to defend itself from such cancers for posterity sake.

THE 'FIVE FINGER' THEORY ILLUSTRATED

The human five fingers has the secret of the posterity of our world—from family to community, community to the nations of this world. Now lift up your hand and take a good look at your five fingers, and then answer the following questions:

1. Are they all equal?
2. Are they all equally fingers?
3. Can the hand function or function effectively if all the fingers were equal?
4. Do they each have peculiar roles to play due to the difference in sizes?
5. Does any of them (no matter how big or small) hold more or less value compared with the rest?
6. Can any of them take the position of another and perform their job effectively?
7. Are they all sitting on the same base?
8. Is there room for each of them on the same base?
9. Are they each independent from one another?
10. Does any impose their will on another or seek to force the rest to become like them?
11. Can the hand function effectively if one of the fingers is weakened or damaged?
12. Can they swap places, irrespective of how they cross over or mix with one another?
13. Did any of them choose their particular location?
14. Was it by accident they each found themselves in their locations?
15. Is it possible that one can deliberately harm or weaken another for

their own gain?

16. What do they do when one of them is accidentally injured and why?
17. Can the hand function effectively if the fingers start fighting amongst themselves?
18. Can any of them fixate itself on self-interest at the detriment of another or the rest?
19. What does it require for the hand to be at its most effective?

The five finger represents our families, communities, and nations in a nutshell. It is likely that everyone has come to (if not the same answers) similar answers. The human fingers tell us everything we need to know about ourselves, others, and the world we each are all renting as tenants. There are no landlords on this earth, irrespective of how many properties we buy or own. We all arrived without knowing who our parents would be or the nation we were going to be born into. Hence no finger chose its location. In the same token, we must all depart for others to occupy and later join us as well. Here are my answers to the above questions, and I hope they are similar to yours. If they are, then we are on the same page and on the right track.

Though all the fingers are not equal, they are all equally fingers sitting on the same base. The hand will either not function or function effectively if all the fingers were equal. Their differences suggest that they have differing and peculiar roles to play for the hand to function well. Their different sizes are critical to their needs and, irrespective of how small or big, none has more or less value compared to another or the rest. What one can do, none else can do effectively. No matter how they cross over, none of the fingers can take the position of another, and there is space for each finger on their shared base. None of the fingers chose its location; they all found themselves in the various locations which were not predestined by them. They never harm themselves but would rather go to protect any that is accidentally injured, in the knowledge that the loss of any would amount to the rest over-compensating and the weakening of the overall efficiency of the hand. They never go into fights because the hand will fail in its duty to the body if the fingers begin to fight amongst themselves.

No finger imposes their will on another or others, and none seeks to make another become like it. Each brings what they have in exchange for what they do not possess in the spirit of mutual cooperation, partnership, respect, unity, and togetherness. For the hand to function at its best, each must be independent, strong, and healthy but must bring their unique attributes and gifts together in one accord for the benefit of each other and one another. In view of this, as individuals, communities, and nations, we must strive to understand and inculcate these as guiding principles but, most importantly, before we think of what to take, we must first think of what to give in exchange.

The root of every finger has to be strong and healthy for them to function to capacity. Any finger whose root is rotten will not be able to produce its quota, and any finger that has an agenda to damage or restrict another finger's root will cause a malfunction or weakening of the hand.

Why and how did human beings subscribe to theories meant for the jungle as in George Orwell's 'Animal Farm' where it was said that 'all animals are equal, but some are more equal than the others'? Jungle justice theories that suggest that life is all about the 'survival of the fittest' and 'winner takes all.' Why, for example, must the 'winner take all' in the world of 'rational' human beings? Can Usain Bolt win or lose any race on his own, irrespective of how fast he is? It takes the loser(s) to make a winner. Therefore, a winner cannot 'take all' when it comes to rational human beings.

If we are indeed rational human beings that we are meant to be, we must know that these theories and sayings belong solely to the jungle in the animal kingdom, because some animals depend on eating others for their survival. Human beings are not in this category, as we are productive, inventive, analytical, and imaginative. If our ancestors who subscribed to this way of thinking knew that these 'jungle justice' way of thinking would lead mankind to this situation today where no one is safe, they would have subscribed to the theory of 'the human fingers,' which has been proposed in the book Humility of the Brain.

In practical terms, those classified as 'black' people, as an example, represent at least two of the five fingers. They occupy the part of the world with the most natural resources (Africa). However, that part of the world remains deprived and dysfunctional as a result of poor governance. A combination of poor leadership and followership has hampered their growth and productivity due to their inability to harness their true potentials. Their collective dysfunctional system is not only due to internal factors but also external factors. However, this malfunction and inability to harness their true potentials is a huge loss shared amongst the rest of humanity and the world. It is impossible for the hand not to suffer and become less effective and productive when one or more of its fingers fails to function or malfunctions. In the same way, it is impossible for the world not to suffer and become less effective when a huge part of it, such as Africa, is malfunctioning.

When one part of the body is burdened, the rest of the body is burdened and suffers. It is only if the remaining fingers are psychopathic in nature would they think they are benefiting from the malfunction of the other finger/s. Those classified as 'Black' people need to realise that their collective backwardness is not only to their detriment but the detriment of the entire world, whilst those classified as 'White' or whatever colours that are ascribed need to realise that 'black' people doing badly is costing them severely in ways they may not understand currently, but eventually humanity will suffer greatly as a consequence. After all, no matter how brilliant one is, they are as good as their weakest link. Others can only take pleasure in the demise of 'Black' people if they are in a psychopathic state, because it is only in this state will people not have insight into how the destruction of others means their own destruction as well.

'Black' people also need to understand that the blame game will not get humanity anywhere but if there should be blame, they must blame themselves for selling first before blaming others for buying during the slavery era, for example. It goes without saying that there will never be a buyer if there was not a seller. No one can rectify an error they have not identified or an error they blame others for. It always takes two to tango.

When a people begin to give awards, titles, and celebrate individuals who have clearly failed, destroyed their families, and stolen individuals' and public funds...when a community is based on the worship of money, that community must and should blame itself first before it blames others. On this same token, if people base their lives on cheating, repressing, and oppressing others, they must also blame themselves first. It is necessary to be self-aware, but there is everything wrong in being self-absorbed and absolving. The cleanliness of a hand depends on the hand washing the other and the other washing it.

In terms of malfunctioning finger/s, if only humanity can imagine and appreciate how its fortunes would positively change when, and if, just three-quarters of resources buried in Africa is harnessed and utilised accordingly. Until those classified as 'black' people and others, as individuals, communities, and nations, harness their unique attributes, build up their economic strengths and pull together in the spirit of mutual respect and exchange (like the five fingers), humanity will remain in darkness in spite of 24 hours, 7 days a week electricity supply.

Why do Africans and those ascribed as black lazily default to God or Satan in things they should own up? Is this a way of absolving themselves of any blame in order to repeat the same mistake? What happened to their God-given WILL?

Why, also, is it that they are the ones visibly expressing sisterly and brotherly love, hugs, and kisses but are envious of themselves and struggle to network and work together?

Be reminded that the failure of those ascribed as blacks to maximise their individual and collective potentials and that of Africa, a continent blessed with the most natural resources, is one of the major reasons our world is malfunctioning. Africa metaphorically represents more than one finger in the equation and formation of this world we are all renting. Think of what would happen to the hand in relation to its effectiveness, efficiency, and survival when more than one of its fingers malfunctions. Does it take a rocket scientist to understand this? Any individual, community, or nation that sees anything good in this or thinks it benefits them needs urgent psychological attention, because humanity is paying an awful price for this malfunction.

The main problem preventing this from happening is 'Psychopaths and Sociopaths' from different corners of the globe. Irrational psychopathic and sociopathic tendencies lie beneath the entire problem humanity is going through, because the foundations upon which the current occupants/tenants of our world are building are laid by psychopaths and sociopaths with concepts, ideologies, and theories meant for the jungle. Rational means when one can sacrifice ... when one sees and acts objectively beyond selfish and vested interest for the common good of humanity. What would the hand gain in the end if it consumes everything to the detriment of the leg? What would happen to the hand in the end of the leg dies or starts to malfunction?

Let it not come as a surprise that the survival of our world will owe much to the survival of Africa. The continent with the most in natural resources of which many remain untapped. The survival of Africa will also hugely depend on what happens in Nigeria, Africa's most populous nation endowed with natural resource and whose citizens perform excellently on an individual basis but are woeful collectively as they cannot network or work in partnership. However, and above all, the survival of our world rests with the girl child who is the womb carrier and later the mother of the future of our world (children). Having said all that, the real survival of the world depends on all who are renting it, for every individual, community, and nation is unique with peculiar attributes to bring to the equation. The helping hand humanity is in dire need of lies with the hand itself through the 'Five Finger' theory. The independence, individual identity, and attribute of each finger, coupled with their mutual respect, partnership, unity, and collective responsibility. Though they are independent, they all remain interdependent on one another and each other.

The major problem is that humanity has been, and remains, very confused and ill-informed about the world. The confusion has led it to look in all the wrong places for answers. Humanity concentrates more on the four walls of the classroom to provide it with leaders. It seeks out those with academic intelligence, material and financial clouts to be custodians of the 'right way' of doing things, relies heavily on science and technology designed by 'man' who is limited, politics, and at times misguided religion to provide all the answers.

Humanity depended primarily on men for leadership, but men laid the dangerous foundations in terms of concepts, theories, and ideologies that damaged and continue to damage this world to date, when women are more naturally equip when it comes to multitasking and distribution. If one must choose then, women are more important because they are the source of life. Just like humanity wrongly focuses and gives more attention to physical health without knowing that mental health is more important to physical health, they make the same mistake with men and women. Therefore, I say, to hell with 'Gender Equality,' for no two women are equal, let alone a woman and a man. Just like the five fingers, we are all different for a reason.

Humanity also focused on Europe and America primarily; at worst, either suppressed or, at best, negating places like Africa, which is the continent with the most natural resources. Humanity failed to appreciate that if there's anything called 'more important,' then Africa could be that—because of what lies beneath Africa in terms of natural resources compared to other continents. Having said all that, the critical thing to note as it relates to the importance of women and Africa is that, 'no matter how important or big a part of the engine is, it can never function on its own, and as little as a plug is, it can render a massive engine useless.'

Humanity has also focused on the arrival of saints to resolve all the problems without knowing that this world is not compatible with saints and, to date, no one has been able to 'cast the first stone.' Humanity has not quite understood the difference between sin and crime, and the fact that sin is not primarily responsible for the evils of humanity, but crime is. Sin remains something no one is immune from. Hence I say, "If I were righteous, I would not go anywhere near a place of worship" (Ihenacho 2014), because I don't want to be exclusive or special. I only attend because I go to meet fellow sinners, strugglers, and seeking to do better.

Valuing and harnessing each person's, community's, and nation's attributes and resources are critical to the survival and posterity of humanity. 'Independence' and the development of each is the right cause of action, but it should incorporate the right motives with the spirit of collaboration, partnership, and togetherness, because this is one world, one entity, and one human race. None should be preferred at the expense of another; rather, mutual respect and mixture of approaches are key. Having said that, independence is, and will, remain an illusion, because no individual, community, or nation can survive on their own. We will remain interdependent on one another and each other in this one world we are all renting as tenants. There are no ifs, and there are no buts!

Each country being independent, healthy, and strong but coming together in one accord, with each bringing their unique attributes (like the five fingers), is the only way forward. It is necessary for each country to harness all its potentials and pursue its interest as long as such pursuit of national interest is not to the detriment of another or other countries. The chaos in our world today is because countries are going against this rational principle and they are aggressively pursuing national interests at the expense of others, without realising the long-term damaging impact on humanity as a whole. Observe your five fingers and ask, "What will happen to the hand if the fingers embark on such mission as human beings?"

Keep in mind that the hate of one on the grounds of differences of any kind is the hate of self, because the hater is also different; no two persons are same, and each has a unique and vital contribution to make for the posterity of humankind.

Humanity needs to wake up and wake up fast. One does not need to be a rocket scientist or wizard to anticipate what is on the horizon for humanity. An in-depth reflection will reveal impending disaster when one considers the interplay between the level of hazardous materials at the disposal of human beings and the level of emotional decadence generating hatred in humanity against itself. The contrast is likened to "placing a fully loaded machine gun in the hands of a five-year-old" (Ihenacho 2014).

Every individual, community, and nation needs to activate themselves and be the best they can be for the posterity of humanity. Your slumber and backwardness are not only detrimental and costly to you but humanity in general, because you are the reason I am here and I am the reason you are here. We need each other; therefore, as I give the best I can, you need to be at your best in order to give your best too. Hampering any is hindering others; hindering self is depriving others. Any finger that fails will automatically create more jobs for the rest and weakens the overall efficiency and effectiveness of the hand. The perceived benefits from another's, or others' failings are costly to everyone in the long run. It is one world and one entity. Any damage to one part will inadvertently, and adversely, affect the rest in ways never imagined.

If only one can imagine who or what they are, what they would become, what the world would look like, what they would do or how they would feel if they wake up one morning and all they can see is only themselves and no one else.

All the fingers need to be activated so they can maximise their unique potentials they are together in one accord for the hand to function at its best. As big and as useful as any finger, it is useless on its own. If one thinks the brain is very smart, they should separate it from the body and see how useless it becomes. The brilliance of a smart brain can only be seen and felt when it cohabits, collaborates, and works in partnership with other effective and efficient parts of the body. Let's subscribe to the 'Five Finger' theory and its principles in order to see the beauty of humanity. The time to save humanity is now! It is critical to remind humanity and emphasise that no individual, community, or nation can attempt to, let alone go it alone and survive. It's time for reflection and change for the posterity of humankind.

Now hear the words of wisdom from Michaelene Gail Holder-March's grandmother who said, "Our hands are the most important part of our anatomy; it enables us to express deeply held emotions which can be love, indifference, or hate."

Globally, hand gestures vary significantly across religions, cultures, and countries.

Hand movements sometimes can reveal our deep and hidden thoughts, therefore, betraying subconscious thinking. The human hand is the primary agent that brings the thoughts in one's head into action. However, the power of the hand lies in the fingers as they can signal accusatory, demand silence, offer love, and give warnings, but a dearly departed grandmother Louise Victoria Grace Holder, otherwise known as "Waxy" from Grenada West Indies, once said, "The fingers when held by another signalled strength and unity, only if each finger participated in the grasp. The thumb indicates respect for each other; index finger is trust followed by understanding, affection, and compassion." Take any of these out, and the hand would lose a vital component that can never be replaced. Though the hand may continue to function, it would not function at its best. This is applicable to humanity; therefore, it is not rocket science that our world is terribly malfunctioning.

When humanity understands and appreciates the 'Five Finger' theory, it will come to the realisation that the person who sold their birthright and the one who bought it are confused, wrong, and equally guilty. This is because they are both partakers in the malfunction seen in humanity. In accordance with the principles of the 'Five Finger' theory, being big or small and being different does not imply that any finger is superior or inferior, or more or less important than others, because each has a unique role and contribution to make to the overall effectiveness of the hand.

The differences seen in the five fingers are there for complementary and collaboration purposes, not for competition, challenge, or popularity contest. The five fingers also remind us that we, human beings, are not equal, and will never be equal, but are, at the same time, equally human beings. We just need to appreciate and respect each other's differences, then activate each and ensure everyone performs to their respective maximum ability so that the hand can be at its best.

In view of the above, we, human beings, renting this world for only a season need to adjust our thinking quickly and stop subscribing to old, misguided, ill-informed, and irrational ideologies, concepts, and theories of our ancestors, and embrace the truth for our posterity. This is our only option; otherwise, we are heading towards disaster, if we are not there already. This is a clarion call, but it remains obvious that a confused brain would act confused, because a goat cannot bark, neither can an iron bar produce water.

Wisdom can only come from the wise, and only the wise can understand, recognize, and appreciate wisdom. Nothing in life is for everybody, and as fruits on top of a tree, we cannot all ripen at the same time. These notwithstanding, the time to save humanity is now.

We are not here in this world to conquer or concede; we are here to contribute and complement. Though we share certain similarities with other animals, we, as human beings, are very different from other animals. We are intellectually lesser and more vulnerable than other animals at birth. Nature has literally very little to offer us in terms of our survival and posterity at birth. However, we are born with the ability to become rational through adequate nurturing. Our shortfall in reaching the adequate height of nurturing or even understanding this has led to our irrationality, as we retained a great chunk of the animalistic instincts. This is why we have progressively gone astray, as we continue to build on old and poorly laid foundation by our forbearers. We have it in us to reverse this awful trend, starting with the understanding, appreciation, and implementation of the 'Five Finger' theory.

CHICKEN & EGG IN HUMANITY RESOLVED?

Though nature is mainly responsible for the human species' arrival, sustenance (which still has a strong element of nurture), and departure, it has nothing much to offer human beings in way of survival and/or posterity. Other species in the animal kingdom are hugely favoured and more likely to survive based on the offerings of nature, but human beings are less so. A puppy, for example, can walk within minutes and locate its feeding source, recognise danger, and become aware of its carer.

Between three and four years of age, a chimpanzee becomes totally independent of its mother and can defend and protect itself in the harsh wild. Once independent, they have no need for their parents and do not need to return home if things do not work out. A three to four-month-old Ape has a grip an adult human being may not possess. But a human baby will die if left to the devises of nature without the protection of an adult carer.

No baby would have been able to find its feeding source or identify its mother at birth. It takes, at the very least, a month before a human baby's sensory organs click into gear. A human baby would need practical nurturing to remain alive and survive. At six months, a human baby is not able to recognise the danger posed by a Lion or fire and would drop into a hole without guidance, but a puppy would not.

Nurture is mainly responsible for human posterity and survival. Therefore, it is impossible for any baby to be able to feed itself within a six-month period or be able to recognize, let alone run away from danger in one year. No child will be able to become independent of an adult at the age of three. No child will ever be able to brush their teeth, clean their room, or even say good morning without being taught consistently and constantly. Other animals are quick to recognise their main carers and cling to them, but also quick to disconnect completely, and from them, once liberated in adulthood, but human beings are very slow to recognise their parents in infancy—but once recognised, they never, under normal circumstances, forget.

Now, forget about all the theories we were born to read about, accept, modify, or use but focus on the fact that the gestation period of human foetus stands at approximately nine months. Focus also on the fact that this is what we all know, which has been, and will remain so, irrespective of whether the womb bearer is located in the most deprived or affluent part of our world. Focus on the fact that no human baby would have survived without an adult carer nurturing it, and that human babies are very different from other animals, and though they are born with the potential to be nurtured to the point of rationality, they remain one of the weaker species in both strength and intellectual ability at birth. They are the most helpless, hopeless, and vulnerable.

In view of these, it is obvious that it took two adults (male and female) for the conception of a human baby, and it took an adult, at the very least, to nurture that baby to independence; else, it would have died. Therefore, as far as human beings are concerned, and based on the available unequivocal evidence, the Chicken laid the egg. If this is the fact, can it be logically true that other animals came the same way? Even though similarities and differences from one species to another are there for all to see, human beings are the only species able to defy the rules of nature. No other animal can do this without human beings contributing to it.

In the animal kingdom, it is noticeable that certain animals look more alike compared to others. This can be seen in goats and sheep, small cats and big cats, ape and human beings, for example. Human beings need to be clear that as Sheep and Goats, small Cats and Big Cats look alike, Apes and Monkeys may have been classified as human beings' primates, but they are all on different parallel lines that will, and can, never meet. Apes and Monkeys are born, live, and die as Apes and Monkeys, and human beings as human beings. There has never been, and will never be, any crossing over.

Nature offers Apes and Monkeys more than it offers human beings, hence at four years of age, an Ape becomes independent of its parents. The 'super creation' is human being. Hence human beings are the only species in the entire animal kingdom that are endowed with the power and ability to be both imaginative and creative. Apes and Monkeys are unable to bring human beings in for experiment or any special study, but human beings can do this at will. This, coupled with the fact that no human baby can survive without an adult carer's nurturing, gives credence to creation.

Even if there was a 'big bang,' wouldn't something be responsible for the 'big bang,' because every reaction stems from an action of some sort? In view of the fact that human beings are the only species heavily dependent on nurture, is it not then misguided to apply or be governed by natural theories such as 'survival of the fittest' and 'winner takes all, dog eat dog' that are meant for other animals primarily governed by nature? And according to George Orwell in his book Animal Farm, "All animals are equal, but some are more equal than the others." Aren't all these theories that should be applicable and compatible to the rules of the jungle? The jungle is where some animals depend on eating others for their survival.

In view of what we categorically know, the 'one million years evolution process' sounds like a gimmick fit for story books, because no one lives that long to observe the process. It is obvious, from what we know about the gestation period of a human foetus and the developmental stages of a human baby, that two adults were responsible for any baby born, and had to nurture the baby to live. If this is so, is it not possible that other animals went through the same process? If indeed there were an adult that gave birth to the first baby or babies, then the question would be: How did those two adults come about? Though the evolution theorists did not categorically claim that human beings evolved from Apes, many have been derailed to assume and think that. To those, I say, if such evolution took place, why did that process stop? And if it is still on-going, then where are the next Apes about to become human beings or human beings going the other way?

No Ape can live long enough to evolve into anything else, and so is a human being. Why is that type of evolution only applicable to Apes and human beings? Which animal did Goats, Lions, Sheep evolve from? Every animal, including humans, is different and on specific parallel lines that never cross over or meet, even though they may have originally come from the same source. It is an acceptable theory that all animals came from the same source. This means that the source from whence human being came is the same source all other animals came.

Getting that source as right as possible is critical, because when one gets their past wrong, they are likely to get their present and future wrong too. This is the truth; it is not theory. If one wants to challenge this, it must not be on the premise of 'whose truth' as 'confusionists' would say. It should be on projecting their perceived subjective truth for debate, at the very least. Let's get real as human beings; else, we remain confused and perish.

How come it is only the human species that has to depend on nurturing for its survival and posterity, and the rest of the animal species, including Apes and Monkeys, are favoured more by nature, even though they require nurturing too?

If an offering of nature, such as water, which is friendly to every living thing and source of life, can be hazardous to human beings when stretched or used in excess, then everything made by imperfect and limited human beings will not only be limited but extremely toxic when fixated and/or depended upon to a great extent. Understanding the limitations of man-made science, technology, religion, capitalism, political correctness, and academic education is critical to humanity's posterity and survival.

Human beings need to call to mind that they are the least favoured be nature in terms of survival. They are one of the species, if not the only species, that will never survive based on the offerings of nature. They are the only species that come into existence totally useless, needy, helpless, and empty and stay that way for months, if not years. Therefore, they must depend on nurture for their survival. However, with their decapitated limitations in their early years comes the potential to rule over all things, including more physically powerful beasts of the earth.

They are bestowed with the potential to become rational, live in peace and harmony by going through three stages of nurturing. Unfortunately, they are more in tune with two out of three stages of nurturing, which leave them with a chunk of their animalistic instinct. Hence they malfunction as human beings.

The world is littered with an abundance of resources and spacious enough to contain double the number of people currently inhabiting it. But humanity has struggled and continues to struggle because it has remained irrational due to its failure in recognising and/or implementing the three stages of nurturing required. As a result of this, human beings are witnessing a world full of irrational acts that stem from irrational thought processes by irrational and ill-informed human beings. It is in recognition of these facts that the 'Five Finger' theory was born for the posterity of humanity. It was also as in recognition of these facts that this book came into being.

All humanity asks of all individuals, religious groups, communities, and nations is: act like candles and stars. As candles, they will go about losing nothing but gaining a lot from lighting other candles. And as stars, they go about doing their work, and even if they know their worth, they never refer to themselves as stars; rather, others see their work and proclaim them as stars.

Everyone should focus and continuously work on their limitations and leave others to point at works and praise them for their strengths. Even stars are 'aware' that they cannot do the job of the sun and the moon. As important as stars are, they are 'aware' of their limitations. Any star that goes about proclaiming to be a star is fake and grandiose. As such, any individual, religious group, community, or nation that does the same is grandiose, irrational, and working against humanity. The sign of a malfunctioning mind is a mind that feels it knows everything and speaks of its wisdom and courage. A sound mind speaks of humility amidst praise and adoration.

I am delighted to say that I have seen and acknowledged such individuals in the acknowledgement section of this book. It is my wish to acknowledge the source (parents, particularly the mothers) from whose womb those individuals came, because it was that source that laid the foundation for them through adequate nurturing.

INSPIRATION!

Inspiration is what, if not everyone, most people are seeking at times, without knowing that there's no bigger or better way to be inspired than the discovery of self-worth, purpose, and understanding of the mechanics of this transient life. This is the base upon which all else is based and built. It is the starting point; else, destruct awaits anything built without this base or this foundation. When one understands where they are coming from and their current location, their destination becomes a formality.

Now, consider that if you are 100-year-old, it means that a hundred years ago you, like me, arrived into a strange world without knowledge of the carrier of the womb or the nation you stepped in from. You came in just like me, totally empty and without preconceived ideas about anything or anyone. All you could do then was to cry when in need, wet yourself, and you were totally dependent on others for your feeding, clothing, health, safety, and security. You gradually began to make sense of a very strange world based on observation, imagination, and trial of things you saw and/or heard from others. You began to develop your own personality and ideologies by replicating, minimising or enhancing those acts seen or heard.

As you enhanced based on your personality, you may have reinvented or recreated things, but everything you have achieved is based on already existing principles. This is because no one would have thought about flying without seeing the birds of the earth. It is intriguing to note that birds of the earth were not an invention of man. It is also a well-known fact that no living thing, including man, can exist or survive without water, and water also is not an invention of man. The same is applicable to the air we breathe and many other things man cannot make.

It is critical to know that, irrespective of what you and I reinvent, we can only know so much, and due to the fact that you and I are limited, all our inventions in the areas of religion, politics, capitalism, science, and technology, for example, WILL remain subject to limitations. Therefore, over-reliance on any of these will become futile and hazardous to humanity.

It is because you can only know so much and, irrespective of how much you know, they would serve as only a part of the jigsaw puzzle, which means nothing without other people's parts coming into play. Hence we are all different. This is the vital lesson of the 'Five Finger' theory reinvented in England as a component to the posterity of humankind. It is my take that humanity only reinvent, because we build on existing principles—nothing comes out of nothing. When we appreciate this, it would restructure our brains and bring us to a state of humility and grace. We do not necessarily need to love everyone, but respect should be non-negotiable from person to person, religious group to religious group, community to community, and nation to nation. I need to respect myself for who I am and respect you for who you are that I am not, as the job of a cleaner is as important as the job of a prime minister, even though they are on different pay scales.

Remember, as limited as you and I were on arrival, so will we be (life permitting and nature taking its course), as we approach our respective departure gates from a world we must leave behind for other occupants.

Ladies and gentlemen, boys and girls, it has been said that in our world today, some believe that one day science and technology will find answers to death. This has led a few people to either pay or take up insurance to pay in order to have their lifeless or dead bodies preserved, waiting for the dawn of such a period. It is my wish to remind such people and others intending to embark on such a scheme that science and technology are inventions of 'limited' human beings, and every invention of one who is limited will also be limited.

If science can revive those whose bodies are preserved at the dawn of such a period, how would it revive those whose bodies died in ghastly accidents or burnt to ashes by fire? How would science locate those whose bodies may not be found or have been eaten by wild animals? Or is it only those whose bodies are preserved that would be revived? At that time, would science stop people from dying in ghastly accidents, fire or people dying alone and only being found when their bodies are decomposed? Without discouraging human endeavours and search for answers, in a mysterious world, isn't part of our strengths understanding of our limitations? I have continuously stated that as useful as anything, including water, when used or stretched beyond its limits, it would become hazardous to humanity; as such, why then would people continue to donate their vital organs in order to save lives when there is hope of being revived? And, would this not hamper the advancement of science when everyone is in pursuit of this adventure of being revived?

I am inspired to ask of humanity to consider the following: how come the weakest, the most helpless and vulnerable on arrival later become the strongest? How come the most dependent, weakest physically and intellectually on arrival can, at a later stage, bring the strongest in for analyses and studies, but the strongest cannot do it? How on earth is it that a visitor and stranger can lay claim of ownership to a world that was here before their arrival and a world that would remain here on their departure? How come it is only human beings and no other species in the entire animal kingdom can do these, including Apes?

The journey of my soul

Amongst the little gifts and messages given to me to deliver to humanity is this: it is impossible that all will either agree or disagree. I know there's someone, somewhere waiting for this message. Hence I am compelled to deliver it and make it part and parcel of this book. Please read and judge for yourselves and make what you will out of it. That's what freewill, differing thought processes, and choices is all about. Do, however, remember that my thoughts are different, so are yours. Just like different parts of an engine, our different thoughts are there for complementary purposes, because none is complete on its own. None is more or less important than the other. This is not rocket science; however, an irrational mind will struggle to understand this unequivocal and uncontestable fact. Humanity is in dire need of this understanding, for the time to save humanity is now!

Though loving one another is mandatory from religious perspective, it is not desirable from secular world perspective. What should be mandatory from all perspective is RESPECT. Respect for self and others, respect for differences and different attributes, opinions, and beliefs, so long as they speak of collaboration, complement, and partnership. The creator is all for differences. Hence we have the unequal but equally important fingers. Anything that seeks to uniform all things is ungodly, immoral, and inhumane. Respect is the most vital ingredient for the posterity of humanity.

In view of this, I respect those who believe in God, irrespective of the channel they use to get to God. I also respect those who do not have any belief. The little I have been so privileged to know about God is that our God chose us amongst the rest, including Angels and Apes, and made us gods. The only difference between God and us ... the only thing or limitation God put in place is that none of us, as individuals, can be god on our own, but only He alone is God on His own!

How did God make us gods?

All other species, including Apes, Monkeys and even Angels, were spoken into existence. Only human beings were created and made by God's hands, in His image, and with His breath inside us came the free will to even rebel against God. God laid all the principles, invented and created all things. However, with His breath inside us and the free will, we were given the power to recreate and reinvent. Hence every reinvention of 'man' is based on existing principles and with limitations. The floor upon which we build anything isn't ours, neither are the birds of the earth which inspired our flying ability.

The power to do wonders, both good and bad, is in every child, irrespective of whether they believe or not. This power has been the driving force in many scientists who oppose God, but scientific research and work is a typical example of the gods and the free will we possess. The only difference, as I indicated earlier, is, no matter how good a scientist, no scientist can achieve anything on their own. Any rational and wise scientist would be the first to acknowledge how useless, helpless and vulnerable they are on their own. As good and powerful as science is, no reinvention or recreation of man, including religion, capitalism, politics, is without limitations, because 'man' by its very nature is limited.

Therefore, none of these, including science, is in competition with God or creation; rather, they are those exploits human beings were given the power and free will to perform.

The power of recreation has led 'man' to bring wild beast (physically more powerful than man) and tame them to do things that are not natural for them. We have the power to bring Apes in for study, but no animals out there can do this to us. The power to reinvent enabled human being to develop the idea and build an aircraft by looking at the birds of the earth. As weak, helpless and as vulnerable as we come compared to other species, every 'normal' human baby comes with the ability to recreate and/or reinvent, but would never be able to do it on their own. The only power all possess and able to do automatically and naturally is the power and free will to do bad. Hence a two-year-old child can scatter a room without instruction or teaching, but could require a lifetime to learn how to arrange the same room.

Every 'normal' baby is like a new fully furnished property with every gadget available. Because none can be god on their own, if those around the baby, including the baby's respective society, fail to help the baby activate those gadgets, they could remain dormant and wasted inside that baby, and the baby would not only lose out but humanity will, too, in ways that one cannot comprehend. It is this negligence by those around the children of this world we are all renting, and society at large, that is responsible for the shame of humanity.

Do pray and do fellowship, but remember, God is saying: "Love me with all your heart, soul, and strength, and love one another, but what you are asking Me, I have already given you, even those of you who have turned against Me. Look at those called scientists, some of them have turned against Me, but they would keep on doing exploits by activating and following the principles of working together, which enables the recreation and reinvention abilities I have put in each an everyone of you as gods. However, no one is capable of activating these principles on their own. Hence, success is not something any of you can achieve on your own. When, it is said in the Holy Books, 'When two or three are gathered in My name...,' it simply means, when two or three are gathered and agree, the god implanted in each of you is activate. Therefore, whatever the two or three sincerely agree upon and are determined to do whether good or bad; the free will I have given you all will make it come through.

Every baby comes into the world empty. I have made only failure available to each of you, so you do not have to do anything to achieve it. Now, say the Lord's prayer, praise, worship, and glorify Me but then look within you, network, compliment, collaborate, and work in partnership with one another and see that I have already made you gods with My hands, put my breath into you, and given you the free will to do exploits, but not on your own." With these, let's awaken our spirits in the quest to save humanity.

Who is a human being?

Any living being with the ability to read, write, reflect, project, bear a name and be able to name names is a human being. Such living being, under normal circumstances, will be able to remember, maintain contact, or retain links with their particular lineage following independence and for as long as life, health, and other social factors permit. Such living being can recreate, reinvent, and put things in motion. They can also cause other animals to do things they are not naturally meant to do, but no animal out there can tame or bring in a human being for studies. These are abilities only the human species possesses and no other species in the entire animal Kingdom have, including Apes and Monkeys.

Just like cars are cars, irrespective of make or model, and the quality of the contents of each vehicle is not determined by its looks, size, make or model, so are human beings. Human beings, irrespective of their differences which are there to enhance and benefit them, and their contents and qualities, are not determined by looks, shapes, or sizes. If one cannot see bits of themselves in someone else amidst their differences, then there's a problem with the person's thinking and reasoning.

The baseline is that we all arrived into this world as strangers and stay on it as visitors who must exit once our respective, invisible individual tenancies expire. Think! Whatever you represent to your relatives is likely to be what the other person represents to theirs. In spite of our differences, we come from one source and rent one entity called the world. Just like leaves, different branches, trunks, and stems linked to one root that makes a tree. Human beings are those who may have different accents (like the Scots have different accent compared to English) but cough in a similar fashion.

HOW RATIONAL ARE HUMAN BEINGS?

The things that are synonymous with every 'normal' child are the ability to play, eat, sleep, and scatter things. These activities are natural; they are the rules and practices of life. Hence many animals in the animal kingdom do these, and they are activities that do not require teaching and/or learning to perform. Nature is the source of many, if not all, of the activities anyone can do, hence such activities are not paid for. All the activities like reading, tidying up, and cooking that differentiate human beings from other animals are nurtured activities orchestrated by human beings.

As stated, human beings rely heavily on nurture for their survival and posterity. As irrational and empty as they are on arrival, they have the capacity to become rational. However, in order to become rational, three stages of nurturing is required. At the baseline of these stages is the inculcation of the 'Five Finger' theory. This should run concurrently with the process of nurturing human babies to do daily domestic chores.

The significance of the 'Five Finger' theory, as it relates to human being, needs to be inculcated prior to attaining academic education. If this does not happen, disaster awaits as human beings retain a chunk of their animalistic instincts, though at varying levels, depending on personalities and backgrounds. It is difficult for a human being to become rational based only on the ability to look after themselves and attain academic excellence.

Until human beings become rational, they are likely to retain and/or adopt rules and practices suitable for the jungle which are hazardous to humanity. Being rational means that one can, at all times, metaphorically be in another person's shoes, without having to wear it. Being rational means an understanding and implementation of the 'Five Finger' theory, as contained herein and in the book entitled Humility of the Brain written in defence of humanity (Ihenacho 2014). It means having the understanding that best and worst have no colour, creed, gender, class, status, age, nationality, or language. Only a rational mind would know that wisdom comes from different sources, but an irrational mind restricts and/or deludes itself by thinking it can only teach, learn, and share from a particular source or group of people.

A rational mind would relate to how they entered into this world and appreciate their status as a visitor and tenant who must vacate and not claim ownership of a world they must leave behind. A rational mind would not mask its ills but would acknowledge them and help others, especially children, to learn from them and not go on to repeat the same or worse mistakes. A rational mind would, at all times, seek and pursue the truth, even at own detriment. However, one should remember that somebody holding one truth does not equate to holding all truths, and vice versa.

A rational mind adopts the spirit of appreciation of the invaluable need for differences in humanity, without subjecting it to the deluded concepts of dominance, superiority, and inferiority. An understanding that no matter how important someone is or purports to be, the person can only represent a useful part of a jigsaw puzzle that becomes useless on their own.

A rational person understands that as important as the brain is to the body, it cannot function without the participation of other body parts, and it would be weakened once any or other parts of the body is weak. Being rational makes one complete as a human being who has an understanding that if violence is not tolerated in the home, it cannot be tolerated elsewhere; it also helps one compromise their comfort and pleasure for the sake of that which is right and proper. A rational mind will, at all times, ask, “What have I done for you or them lately?” before asking, “What have you done for me or us lately?”

In this world of plenty, both in size and natural resources, a rational mind would know that human beings are born with the ability to be nurtured to the point of rationality, but very few get to, and have gotten to, that point. Hence humanity is malfunctioning. Many people have no clue what being rational means; some think academic education and being able to look after themselves and their environment qualifies them as rational, and some are confused with the strong belief that human beings are born to behave like animals.

A restricted and irrational mind is a confused and fixated mind dangerous to humanity, as it has no insight into anything they are doing or have done wrong. An irrational mind, like a child, believes that their father is the strongest man on earth; their mother, the best cook on earth, and anything to do with them is the best. An irrational mind places self above all else, and do not know that the self would not exist without the other or others. An irrational mind is unaware of consequences and believes in immediate gratification, not delayed satisfaction. The 'here and now' is always preferred to 'slow and steady planning and execution in order to get things structurally right' to the irrational mind. An irrational mind ignores peculiarities and does things because others are doing it, irrespective of consequences.

It is vitally important that human beings appreciate that, irrespective of background, nobody came into this world with preconceived ideology, concept, or theory. Just like benefactors and inheritors, we all benefited and inherited existing faulty ideologies, theories, and concepts laid down by our fore-bearers who were afraid, less exposed, and driven by forces of nature, which are not compatible with rational human beings. All human beings have done is to continue building on these faulty foundations whilst papering over the cracks. A clever and rational child would soon realise that this inherited building would collapse and destroy all that is in it if they continue to build on these faulty foundations. Such clever child would come out and do whatever it takes to introduce new and solid foundation for a better building to safeguard the health and safety of all inhibitors of this building, which represents the one world.

Humanity has suffered greatly because of failure to adequately understand and challenge these jungle theories which were wrongly incorporated into human existence as a result of irrational thought process. This has caused 'a car that supposedly should run perfectly on four wheels to limp along on three or fewer wheels.' It is in recognition of this fact that the 'Five Finger' theory, which is a theory suitable for rational, reflective and projective human beings, was born.

In order to be rational, here are the three stages of nurturing that every baby needs to go through in more details: 1) nurture in order to understand the principles of the five finger theory and effectively incorporate it into day-to-day activities, because no matter how brilliant anyone, any community, or nation is, they become useless on their own; 2) nurtured to carry out domestic and self-care tasks, because no child, irrespective of background, will ever be able to brush their teeth, clean their room, or even say good morning without being taught; and 3) nurture in order to undertake academic task–for example, no child will be able to read a book or attend school without being taught how to say alphabets in their own language. With these in place, humanity becomes primed to reach the stage of being rational.

Being rational means appreciating that the health and safety of one's children depend on the health and safety of their neighbour's children. As a rational parent, your children should not be under any illusion that you want them caught the same way you want another child who commits a crime caught. Being rational means having the ability to recognise that as good as the brain is in relation to the human body, it can only serve as a part of the jigsaw puzzle and will be completely useless if other parts of the body do not cooperate and work collaboratively in partnership with the brain.

A rational mind wouldn't need to be told that the colour of a horse does not make it more or less of a horse, and same applies to human beings. Being rational also means having a practical implementation of the 'Five Finger' theory in the day to day living, and a clear understanding that no matter how big, good and effective a hand is, its cleanliness depends on it washing the other hand and the other hand washing it. However, the ultimate level of being rational is when one can spare a thought for the other/s, feel sorry, and help those who feel the need to dominate, subdue, and weaken others to realise the damage they are doing to themselves in the process without knowing. These are usually those who subscribe to the concept of superiority and inferiority and, directly and wrongly, relate these concepts to unequal but equally important fellow human being. Such individuals, religious groups, communities, and nations struggle to appreciate that the job of a cleaner is as important as the job of a president or prime minister, even though there are different pay scales. The quantity of petrol consumed by a lorry does not make it more or less important than a smaller vehicle. Such people also fail to appreciate that a Bishop needs the congregation more than the congregation needs the Bishop, because the congregation can worship on their own but a Bishop will not only depend on the congregation for their upkeep but also would face being detained for mental illness if they carry-on on their own without the congregation.

In order for any individual to become rational, the 'Five Finger' theory and its principles need to form the basis of the nurturing process. It also needs to form part of early learning in schools. This is not only necessary but critical because that can help moderate those who would otherwise become grandiose, inferior, or superior as a result of their academic illiteracy, academic excellence, temporary high or low positions in life, and material possessions.

The understanding of all these would make a rational mind appreciate the value and importance of the girl child, who is the main agent to inculcate this in a child. The girl child being the womb carrier would soon become the mother who, life permitting, would not be absent at the birth of her baby. The mother who, (health and social upheavals) permitting, will spend more time with her baby during its formative (0–5) years when the foundation of every child is laid. The child is known to be the future of our world. It is upon this knowledge based on facts that I say, "Men Are The Problem; Women Are The Solution" (Ihenacho 2014).

Without reaching the third stage, humanity will remain in, and retain, a lot of their animalistic instincts, which can make them irrational and more dangerous than wild animals. As stated, human beings are born with the capacity to become rational, but the problem is that very few achieve that and those who achieve that very rarely come close to seats of power. Therefore, most (if not all) of us are irrational but assume to be rational. In our irrational and animalistic state, many delude themselves to think that human beings are like any other animal out there. Many in this weird belief then justify the by-product effects of subscribing and retaining the offerings of nature and not reaching the rational level, which are: greed, selfishness, lack of respect, winner takes all, survival of the fittest, and dog eat dog. The offering of nature which has nothing in it with regards to the posterity and living of the human species but only relevant to animals in the jungle.

How Rational Are You?

As stated, being rational is not an offering of nature. Therefore, it is not a given, as all human beings (though with the capacity to become rational) are born totally empty, helpless, and more vulnerable than other animals at birth. With our world big enough to take double the size of current tenants, well-resourced to carter for its inhabitants, and with the resources not even meant to be shared equally for it to go round, is it not a wonder why humanity is at war with itself? The resources we do not need to share equally because all fingers are not equal. However, no finger should take more than it needs and none should take less than it requires for its sustenance. A mini car should have enough petrol needed to function, and a bus should do the same. The respective amount of petrol consumed by each vehicle does not make one more or less valuable than the other. It does not also equate to the value of their respective contents.

As human beings, we have all manner of hazards confronting us, ranging from illnesses (physical and mental), accidents, natural disasters to death itself, and as such, there is no need for human beings to wage wars on itself based on differences, which is the real source of their survival and posterity.

When one, as an individual, community, or nation, has not reached a level where they subscribe to the principles of the 'Five Finger' theory above and can appreciate that all that is required of them on issues of differences and diversity such as religion, politics, culture, gender, sexual orientation, status, colour, or nationality is to have a discussion. Following that discussion, people can choose to agree, disagree, or agree to disagree. If the decision is to agree to disagree, then they ought not to come back to the same issues unless there is new information to explore; they are still irrational, irrespective of their age, presumed status, academic achievement, or material wealth.

THE 'LIMITED' HUMAN DESIGNED ACADEMIC SYSTEM

Everything in life, both man made and/or natural, is useful but potentially dangerous. Anything stretched beyond its limits will become hazardous to human beings. As natural and useful as water is to every living thing, anyone who drinks water in excess (far and beyond) of what is required will suffer from water intoxication and is subject to die if not treated. It goes without saying that if something as good as water can be hazardous when used in excess, anything made by man, who is limited, must be limited too and hazardous when used in excess. Therefore, any over-reliance on anything made by man, including human designed academic system, capitalism, science, religion, legislation, and political correctness, that is used or stretched beyond its limit will prove hazardous to humankind.

Many things in life have a minimum of two sides. Our human designed academic system is no exception. It has its positive side that is very useful indeed, but the negatives abound. It is easy to see its usefulness, but the destructive aspects of it are incalculable. The shortfalls are incredible to put mildly. In each 'normal' human being, there are, at the very least, two talents embedded, but many have multiple talents. This is why the response one often gets from a child when asked what they would like to be when they grow up is "I am not sure."

Those that devised the human academic systems are the 'evil geniuses' of our world. They created a system that produces brilliant teachers, lawyers, engineers, doctors, scientists, and many other professionals. However, the system also limits the ingenuity of humanity, and with that limitation comes limited opportunities which forces humanity to fight, compete, and challenge, instead of work in a collaborative and complementary fashion. This is part of the reasons many are unhappy in their jobs, because they are doing jobs that have nothing to do with their real calling in life. When one finds their true calling, they are liberated, and from that liberation, they are capable of liberating others.

As important as the limited human designed academic systems, everyone needs to know that, at its best and at its finest, it produces psychopathic and sociopathic individuals. This is because in each expert, based on the offerings of this system, at least three factors seen in Bipolar Affective Disorder patients exist. These are: fixation, mania (of a non-chaotic nature), and grandiosity. One has to be fixated on whatever chosen field they want to be an expert; they have to also be manic about it. They will sleep and wake up thinking about that thing and could deprive themselves and others of many things in pursuit of their dream; otherwise, they cannot fulfil the requirements of being an expert based on this system. Once they achieve their goal of becoming an expert, grandiosity automatically will set in. It does not matter whether they appear humble and subtle with it, deep down they are grandiose, as they are driven by even showing an edge over their contemporaries. If they refused to feel important, others would make them feel important, because they are experts.

To be an expert is a great thing, as humanity needs experts for its posterity. However, the mistake human beings make is to assume that because someone is an expert in economics, law, or science, they are good enough to lead human beings. This assumption is dangerous, as humanity employs people with serious mental health symptoms characterised mainly by grandiosity. In the end, we have leaders who are likely to only see themselves and not give a damn about others. Are we still wondering in view of this fact why our world is in a mess? Is it possible to applaud the managers of this world in view of the terrible mess humanity is in? Don't we judge the taste of the food by eating it? Experts who should be restricted to their areas of expertise and specialism and only drafted in for special advice relevant to their particular field are employed in leadership positions that require a totally different skill sets.

At its best, the limited human designed academic system produces individuals who have psychopathic and sociopathic tendencies capable of masking their inadequacies, incompetence, and mediocrity with eloquent vocabularies and powerful communication skills, 'individuals who are academically too bright for their own good.' These are individuals who often have high levels of energy and drive; it is this energy and drive that they use to drive through their particular interests, irrespective of consequences to others.

It is a system through which the term 'nine to five' was coined. It is a very 'crafty' system that pretends to offer a variety of choices. The choices it offers at the beginning suggests that anyone can be whatever they wish to be, but it very quickly narrows people down to only one thing. In most cases, the one thing it forces people into could be the least of their talents. And, in the end, they are unlikely to be able to extricate themselves from it. It is a system which, by all intents and purposes, created a platform where the 'ninety-nine percent are enslaved by the one percent.' One of the most terrible ingredients of this system is that it is too grandiose and tends to want things in a certain way, and plays superior over all other forms of learning and development. Things have to be presented in a particular way, and people have to reach a particular standard before they are believed to have enough sense. This goes against the rules and forces of nature that accept that nothing is useful on its own.

It is a system that forces many into chasing few opportunities whilst their real potentials are locked and waste away due to the way it is designed. The Human designed academic system rarely appreciates that human beings develop at differing rate and pace. In metaphoric term, IQ testing method is like testing different animals, including squirrels that are experts in climbing trees, with swimming ability. It quickly classifies a squirrel that is an expert in climbing a tree as useless because it could not swim. However, once it narrows those who can perform at an expected level down to a particular career pathway, there is almost no more time to consider or do anything else. By the time one gets home at five, they are exhausted to do anything else until they go back to work the following day. It is not only about the tiredness, but it is also the superannuation entitlements, house rents and mortgage responsibilities, child care, and other responsibilities that tie one down.

Only a handful of people manage to wriggle out of the stranglehold of this system and find their real calling on earth. And when they find their real calling or talent, they become free and more productive to society, as they are likely to liberate others too in the process. The many who are trapped in this awful state are often frustrated and powerless. Their frustration has a crippling effect and impact on humanity, as it destroys the ingenuity of humanity and reduces our overall level of efficiency and self-sustenance/reliance. The system pushes many towards limited opportunities that bring about unnecessary competition and fight as any one job attracts many applicants. This is the real slavery in disguise.

Having said that, it is a fact that this system has proven to produce good doctors, teachers, lawyers, scientists, journalists, social workers, economists, and so on. The system lies beneath all the technological advancement, including sophisticated medical advancement; however, it does not necessarily produce good leaders. For any expert, based on the offerings of the limited human designed academic system, to be a good leader, they would need be in tune with the 'Five Finger' theory and understand the practical implementation of it. Leadership has little or nothing to do with academic sophistication, class, eloquence, or wealth but all to do with wisdom, vision, and common sense.

Leadership is all about providing an enabling environment that ensures that every citizen and community harnesses and maximises their potentials. It is critical to bear in mind that the greatest and most valuable asset known to man is the citizens of this world, human resources (human capital). Anyone or anything that does not recognise this is not fit for purpose as far as leadership is concerned. Anyone with agenda to dominate, suppress, or repress the other or others on the grounds of religion or politics should not be anywhere near the shores of leadership. The terms 'superiority' and 'inferiority' may be relevant to all else with the exception of humanity, where differences is key and where it takes the losers to make a winner. In recognition of this reality, I prescribe that those wishing to become spiritual and/or temporal leaders should subject or be subjected to Mental Health Assessments.

It is worth noting here that, irrespective of what one thinks or whether one is a believer or not, the two most followed leaders known to 'man' since time immemorial are Jesus Christ (Author of Christianity), who is God but came in human flesh, and Prophet Mohammed (peace be upon him), the Prophet of Islam.

The only two things both have in common are: 1) None attended any human designed academic structure. Therefore, they were both academically illiterate; 2) Their backgrounds were littered with abject poverty. One was the son of a carpenter, and the other was an orphan. However, they both possessed gifts of wisdom, vision, and common sense that are sought after to date by many in high and low places.

Humanity has gotten it so wrong by assuming that people without human designed academic education and material wealth have little or nothing to offer. That mere assumption is of huge consequence to humanity, because no one is without consequence. The question here is: Why has humanity restricted itself by being so fixated on something designed by itself, when it should broaden its scope with an understanding that 'every currency has its value'? If humanity will prosper, every individual, community, and nation should, and must count; independence and interdependence must cohabit, and mutual respect must be the order of the day.

The human designed academic system is also flawed in the area of being quick to judge and condemn an individual as being useless. It can shatter a child's confidence and destroy other useful talents and attributes within them. Every human being is a genius, and the genius lives in every child. People must not be judged or condemned based on their ability to undergo academic study. This system negates the fact that human beings develop at different rates and stages in their individual lives based on individual personalities. However, it condemns many so early and traps many others into particular areas where their real purpose in life is not harnessed. This not only generates frustration to the individual but hampers humanity in ways never imagined or understood.

Being super academically educated and/or materially wealthy does not equate to being a good leader. The drive to extreme acts in all spheres of human endeavours, including academics and financial wealth, is often psychotic, characterised by mania and fixated symptoms. Though some people in this state can be useful in their areas of specialism, command a lot of respect because they possess what many do not have, and they are not considered a risk to self and/or others, it does not mean that they are not suffering from mental disorder. Human beings are often overwhelmed by their achievements and wrongly choose such people as leaders.

Leadership is not about how eloquent, academically intelligent, financially rich and elegantly presented one is. Though these characteristics are important, the critical thing about leadership is service to all, not the few. Service that focuses on providing an enabling environment to ensure that the most important and valuable assets (citizens) harness and maximise their potentials individually. Any leader that devises or encourages policies that entrap an individual's or a community's potentials is merely serving as "a goat doing a dog's job" (Ihenacho 2014), and brings ruins to humanity. When any job is given to the wrong person, humanity suffers immensely in ways never to be fully understood or appreciated, especially in the areas of leadership.

We should not worry about an adult who could not give us the correct answer to one plus one; we should, instead, worry about an adult who says, "Does that person look like a bad person to you?" We should also worry more about a parent whose preferred mode of communication is "I don't even care." Never do anything or use anything to trap the genius in you or someone else. When an individual, community, nation, or continent is suppressed or repressed, the genius of individuals within it is subdued. When this happens, it affects the rest of the world adversely, because one can unlock their talent through seeing another person's talent. No one is of no consequence, whether their talent is portrayed or not. Their impact will be felt as a help, or it would hinder humanity. Any dog that goes to a flying competition will be considered useless, but dogs are geniuses in their particular areas of specialism and extremely useful.

Accreditations and empirical research and studies as informed by human-designed academic system are great, but they are not the be-it and end-all. They are also not always factual, because anyone can propose a hypothesis and tailor research questionnaires and data to suit. For some who grew up in families where, at every given time, there's at least up to 60 children growing up with differing behavioural patterns, lived and have seen the world from differing parts and witnessed the contrasting behaviours of dogs that view themselves as meat and those that see themselves as pets, their experiences are factual and unadulterated and vital in addressing the deficiencies in mankind.

When one becomes the experience itself and the news, they will have the limited human designed academic systems playing second fiddle. Therefore, it is more than authentic and does not require a boost from another source. Your voice and your story are invaluable and must be heard, not through a third party but through you. The story is no longer yours, no longer in your interest when someone else—who never felt/lived it, never saw it and never knew it—assumes the position of the storyteller. You lose, but the loss to humanity is greater.

Statistics and surveys can often look plausible but lacking in honesty through massage of information, as one can propose any hypothesis and device questionnaires and data to suit. Therefore, the fact that one is not academic does not mean they are not or will never become a genius in their particular area of human endeavour when developed. Don't rely too much or be deceived by the classroom, because the wisdom of the human designed classroom is subservient to the foolishness of genuine common sense. At times humanity needs the Cock, not the alarm clock, to wake it up.

Never worry much about someone who got one plus one wrong, but worry about an adult who says, 'Does that person look like a bad person to you?' Also worry about those who seek and/or celebrate other people's demise as though they are immune from the afflictions of life. Finally, worry about those who, as individuals, communities, or nations, are in the business of seeking to dominate, suppress, restrict, oppress and devalue others. Those are the irrational beings of the earth, whose actions stemming from their deluded ideologies create enormous pains to humanity. Humanity indeed needs to be rescued at all cost and the time is now.

It is time humanity realises that the liberation of the human mind is the liberation of humanity. A world with approximately seven billion people is being wasteful if it depends on the limited brain of a few who are often 'fixated,' 'manic,' and, at times, 'grandiose,' to survive and these brains are mainly selected based on faulty human-designed academic system. In view of this, I am prescribing a '30-minute rule.' Each of us, like each finger, is unique and has specific role/s to play for the hand to be at its best. This can never be over-emphasised. When each identifies and plays its part in a collaborative pattern well, the beauty and essence of humanity which is founded on our differences are revealed.

Our minds are so powerful there is almost very little it cannot do. Have you got a dream? What is that dream? Have you made it as realistic as it can be in your mind? Do you believe in that dream or are you in doubt? Now think about this and remember this at all times: when your dream is realistic, you need to bring it to a level in your mind where you become passionate about it, even though it might seem unachievable to you. When this happens, you have lit a fire driven by passion. Your only job then is to keep that fire burning and never let it be extinguished by anyone, including yourself. Many will say or do things to create doubt in you about the fire. The last thing you must ensure you did not do is to doubt your dream. Doubting your dream means you have extinguished your fire, and when you doubt yourself, no one will believe you. What your mind says, your body does; there's no two ways about that!

The biggest fraud known to 'man,' following close examination, is what society terms as the '9–5 rat race,' which is primarily a by-product of the human designed academic system. Though it has many positive sides to it, it represents the biggest slavery known to man. It is the corn of our time, because every 'normal' individual has at least more than one talent in them. 9–5, once engaged, has the capacity to trap and enslave the rest of the talents one has.

Now, this is the key to breaking out of that chain. The key is called 'The 30-minute rule.' What 'The 30-minute rule' means is quite simply for everyone to ensure they have, at the very least, 30 minutes each day with their mind only. In this 30 minutes, focus your mind on all the things you think you are good at. List them out one after the other, and gradually narrow them down to 1 or 2. The idea is to bring it down to the one or two things you believe are achievable. Once that is done, then begin to lay the foundation for developing that which you have chosen. Whatever you do, and by all means, have your fears but surmount your fears and never doubt yourself. It is a good thing to have a fear of the unknown, but remember, most of us have restricted ourselves to the 'devil' we know, instead of having the courage to allow the 'angel' knocking and desperate come in, due to fear of failure. Failure is only an opportunity to try again. Trust and invest in your mind to drive you forward in life, for no one can ever fail without their mind saying so.

REASONS FOR THE MALFUNCTION IN HUMANITY

Why won't humanity malfunction when those who are meant to produce and manufacture chose to become and/or are forced to become consumers? Why won't we derail when good and bad that have no colours are falsely defined through assignation of unrealistic colours to human beings, and differences are classified and segregated alongside superiority and inferiority lines and/or projected as vague 'equality' when no two persons are equal but equally important? Why should unrealistic colours be assigned to human beings as a way to define good and bad, when good and bad have no colour?

Why won't we malfunction when differences that ought to propel humanity to greatness have been turned into a source of mistrust, conflict, and suspicion? Why won't humanity struggle when partnership, complement, collaboration, and togetherness are turned into competition, contest, challenge, and divisions when many visitors and tenants to this world everybody is renting assume the delusional position of landlord? And why won't we go into a meltdown when we had incorporated jungle justice theories such as 'winner takes all, dog eat dog, and survival of the fittest' into rational human beings' affairs which should be propelled by the 'Five Finger' theory? Why won't humanity malfunction when it has become over-reliant on limited human-designed academic system which, at its finest, produces psychopaths and sociopaths to give them leaders, hence 'employing goats to do jobs reserved for dogs'? Humanity that's meant to walk and run is being amputated. Humanity that's meant to see is being blinded.

Why won't humanity malfunction when facts are judged based on whose story is sweeter, and when presentation and packaging is worth more than substance? Why won't humanity malfunction when politics is turned into a game, and political correctness means the presentation of a 'spade' in the form of 'bread'? And when many, like the fingers, have lost their worth and/or are subdued, how can the hand function effectively?

In order to catch a lion, one must understand the psychology of lions. It is impossible for anyone to treat an illness they cannot understand. Our world is held at ransom by psychopathic and sociopathic individuals in high and low places—groups, communities, and nations who are pathological liars with high intensity of energy and academic prowess to deceive and confuse. Their games, nature, and language need to be understood in order to offer them the treatment their conditions deserve for their own health and safety and that of others.

One of the symptoms they display and use to confuse many is to attack anything that can destroy their lies. They are like darkness which cannot stand the light. They feed on lies; therefore, frown at anything that's truthful.

Ladies and gentlemen, from this day forward, when you hear someone say, "The truth from your perspective; everyone has what they perceive as their own truth" or ask, "Whose truth?" it is either the person has genuinely been confused by those psychopaths and sociopaths, or they are indeed one of the agents of lies and manipulation whose activities here on earth is to steal, destroy, and kill. Ladies and gentlemen, the truth does exist, hence the 3rd of September 2016 fell on Saturday in England. The liars and psychologically challenged may contest this truth from their subjective platforms for whatever devious or mental state induced reasons; however, there can only be one steady version of the truth. Only lies have different variations and versions. ***The person who needs the truth most remains the person most troubled by it.***

Just remember that the truth will remain that bitter pill responsible for our recovery but difficult to swallow. We need to learn to embrace it for humanity's survival and posterity.

Remember also that war is like jumping into a hole which requires only one step. It is also like cutting a thread with just one strike of the razor or scissors. We can also metaphorically view war as the one hit which occurs in a road accident.

Peace is in the opposite direction of war, as it takes many steps to climb out of a hole if one survives the one step jump in. It also takes some effort to tie up a thread that's cut, and it is almost impossible to retain the same length once a thread is joined up following the cut. Everyone knows the fatalities that can occur and how long it takes to repair a vehicle involved in an accident. It is also certain that some injuries from a road accident stay a lifetime. Bad things come easy, and good ones are a struggle. Let's stop choosing a quick fix and the easy but extremely damaging and costly options.

With all these in mind, humanity needs to think long and hard before severing any relationship from person to person, religious group to religious group, community to community, and nation to nation.

The Deadly Self

The dominance of the 'self' is also at the root of our malfunction. The self, in a metaphoric sense, represents the foundation which, of course, has to be paramount but cannot exist on its own or be accommodating to anyone without the other which represents the structure or building. The 'self' gave rise to terms like personal, individual, and national interests at times, to the detriment of others, are at the base of our confused mindset. The self and the other are for a collaborative and complementary purpose, because one cannot exist without the other. Nothing is destroying families (the bedrock of the world) than the self, and even children are becoming too selfish and self-centred without understanding the importance of the other and others. As important as the self is, it is totally useless on its own, and it is an illusion that one can create happiness on their own without the other or others. The self needs to be put in perspective and arrested for the progression of humanity.

Any individual, community, or nation that is fixated on being interested and concentrating on only themselves within this one body called the world whilst ignoring, negating, or depriving another or the rest has a psychological problem that requires serious and urgent attention. It is not rocket science to know that a malfunction on one part adversely affects the rest in the long run.

It can never be over-emphasised that every individual, community, and nation in this world represents only one hand, and can only serve as one part of the jigsaw puzzle that cannot function without the rest. What is in it for me is a legitimate question that should be asked, but it is more important to ask, What am I offering? It is important to seek added value but only with the intention to add value to the other. It is an illness when all one thinks is what they are getting, what they are taking, but not what they are giving or contributing, no matter how small in exchange. The hidden beauty of humanity is located at the understanding that in order to self-actualise, one has to not only look after self but take care of the other and others. No matter how well behaved anyone's children are, they will remain at risk if their neighbour's children are unruly. Therefore, do not fixate and be absorbed by self.

As important and as powerful as any hand is or purports to be, it can never wash or keep itself clean without the other washing it. We, citizens of this world, need to readjust our thinking for the posterity of humankind. The time to save humanity is now!

Hope for Humanity?

In a world where leaders are being chosen based on how academically intelligent, materially rich, or confused they are, in spite of the fact that extreme academia, material wealth, and confusion of the mind have components of psychopathic tendencies in them...a world where many are not using their real talent and many parts of it have not allowed themselves and/or are being prevented from harnessing their potentials...a world where many high calibre talents are condemned even before they are aware of what they have in them, let alone harness them, due to the criteria set by the limited human designed academic system... a world where controversy is the term used to describe someone who comes close to saying the right thing, and a world where all the primary concepts like capitalism, political correctness, religion, science, and technology have all gone mad; humanity (like a motor car designed to run with four legs tyres has been and continues to run with one tyre) has shown its resilience by limping alone and surviving thus far. The fact that it is limping does not mean it can carry on limping or survive in its current form. However, if it can produce this much with all these malfunctions and limitations, there is hope for humanity if it chooses to correct some of its anomalies. One of the ways to correct the anomalies in humanity is by encouraging opinions.

Opinions!

Having opinions on issues is the greatest gift given to humanity. It is through opinions human beings reveal their thoughts and ideas. Life would have no meaning without expressions of opinion. Things written, said, and done are made possible through opinions.

No opinion is useless, because once expressed, it opens the opportunity for learning for the individual or becomes a gift for another who needs that bit of the jigsaw to flourish. Withholding and/or suppressing opinions are not only detrimental to the individual but detrimental to humanity. Anything that prevents an individual, religious group, community, or nation from sharing their opinion is working against humanity.

Opinions not expressed hinder self and/or others and can manifest in devastating consequences unimaginable and unpredictable. When human beings advance to being rational, expression of wrong opinions would either help the individual to correct their views and, if right, can trigger something beneficial in both the individual and others. Only human beings (and no other animal) have exclusive power to conceive ideas, reflect, and project on them for the manifestation of beauty in humanity. The suppression of these is extremely harmful to humanity, for each has a voice for a reason.

Let's share and cross-fertilise our ideas through the expression of our respective opinions in the knowledge that the worst point we can reach is the point of 'agree to disagree.' As a general guide, expression of the wrong opinion should either mean 'I need help' or 'I'm offering help' when the opinion expressed is right.

THE CORRECT ORDER OF OUR WORLD

As big as any branch of a tree is, it cannot be bigger than the tree itself. In the same way, no individual, irrespective of who they become, should feel bigger than the family they are born into; no family should be bigger than the community it routes from; no community should be bigger than the nation it is located in; and no matter how big, strong, or mighty, no nation should be bigger than this world upon which it is based. There is always a disaster or an impending one when this order is not followed.

The things humanity has to fight for is to secure a just and fair judicial system where every human being is equal before the law and in terms of employment; humanity must resist the temptation of positive discrimination, zoning, and quota systems, as they are all detrimental to it. Humanity needs to, instead, ensure the best suitably qualified and experienced for the job in question. Once this is attained, every other thing is down to communication, negotiation, and compromise. When anyone contravenes the law, the fair and just judicial system will deal with it. If it is a sin, then only the sinless can deal with it. When it is a sin, human beings can rebuke fellow sinner, but no man subject to sinful acts in thought, word, and deed can punish a fellow sinner. Any punishable sinful acts should be made to be part of secular system legislation punishable by the court only.

Humanity needs to stop over labouring itself with things it cannot categorically and unequivocally prove, such as whether or not there's a God. In such issues, the believers in different religious groups and unbelievers should, as a last resort, agree to disagree without condemnation of one another or each other. Keep yours, I keep mine, and we respect each other's position. It is irrational to start disputing or arguing too much on issues of faith. It is also extremely irrational to worship or serve a god that cannot defend itself, let alone protect anyone. Therefore, no one should waste their valuable time worshipping any god they have to protect, defend, or kill for; rather, such gods should worship them. Any god, anything, or person (dead or alive) with special talent or gift without the power to defend itself is nothing but useless. Humanity may but must not argue and fight about things of the spirit in the physical realm.

Humanity should rather focus and concentrate on the hard undoubted facts, such as those that inform it that none knew or will ever know the womb or nation that gave or will give birth to them and the fact that, in spite of our many houses, all of us are tenants renting this world, and must vacate once our individual 'invincible' tenancies lapse. Finally, humanity needs to focus on making itself rational for its posterity and survival.

As human beings, both individually and collectively, we are products of circumstances which make us migrants, no matter where we choose to call home, and ultimately, we are tenants renting this world for only a season. If we cared enough to reflect as rational human beings, we would be in no doubt about this. At the root of migration and asylum lies a bigger picture of everyone of different shades and colour, many highlighting the irrationality of humanity. At times the root causes are ignored whilst fixation at the peripheries takes hold. Delusion is setting a man's house on fire and asking him why he is running. I believe in one world, one human race, humanity, and above all, I believe in one God, the Almighty. I respect those with different belief systems as well as those with none, because everyone is entitled to their own opinions, and without them, I would not have known who or what I am.

When one believes in humanity, they checkmate themselves and those around them in the interest of humanity, but when one doesn't, they act and allow those around them to act like loose cannons at the detriment of humanity. Humanity needs to wake up to reality, for the health and safety of one's child will hugely depend on the health and safety of their neighbour's child.

Homosexuality

The critical thing for humanity to appreciate is that everything said and/or done is driven by mindset and thought process. When the mindset and thought process are right, right utterances and actions follow. On the same token, wrong utterances and actions would be the case when wrong mindset and thought process are in place. In order to act correctly, personal assumptions, subjective feelings, and wrongly conceived cultural and religious dogmas and doctrines should be side-lined.

One needs to be prepared to act in ways that are contrary to their original but wrong feelings and belief systems and suffer personal sacrifice in pursuit of that which is right. With all these in mind, humanity needs to be clear about what it considers as a crime and what it views as a sin. A Victimless crime should not be classified as a crime; rather, when an act has no obvious victim, be it individual or a particular society as victim, but is perceived by some or many as an act that is deviant from the norm, the worst such act can be is sinful or immoral.

Acts of sinful or immoral nature have religious connotations. Homosexuality is one of those acts many from a religious perspective view as immoral and sinful. It is also seen as a deviant act from the norm. Though one can relate to the root cause of these feelings and some of the religious doctrines surrounding these feelings, what is entirely unacceptable is for an act that involves two consenting adults ... an act without an obvious victim to be classified as a crime. For example, it is wrong to view adultery as a crime because it is an act that supposedly involves two consenting adults; rather, it is an immoral act that is sinful in nature. Every living human being has a sinful thing in their life going either in their thought, words, or deeds. The worst any community or nation on earth should do is to condemn and/or ban the promotion of anything perceived by any such community or nation as an immoral or sinful act. That said, communities and nations that want to celebrate and/or promote such acts should be at liberty to do so. In the two opposing sides, none (be it those who promote or condemn such acts) should impose their will on another.

The worst people can do from their opposing positions is to 'agree to disagree,' and thereafter, respect each other's positions until further debate is called, following the availability of new information on the same subject. Issues of morality and sin should only be dealt with in relation to the assignation of punishment by he or she that is holy. Fortunately, or unfortunately, none born of 'man' is holy; therefore, no one alive is qualified to punish sinner, for 'all have sinned and fallen short of the Glory of God.' Furthermore, the owner of the 'vineyard' had instructed that both the weed and crop should be left to grow together until harvest time when He or She would separate the weeds from the crops. It is upon this reason the Sun, Moon, Rain, and Air have no demarcating lines between good and bad people. In view of these, any community, religious group, or nation that prescribes death sentence or any form of punishment for acts deemed as without victims...acts perceived as immoral or sinful is evil, and in the business of hypocrisy, that is detrimental to humanity.

It is critical that each human being on this planet earth appreciates that whether it is through biological factor or by choice, the common denominating factor is every gay or lesbian person is, at best, a human being like the rest of humanity and, at worst, a sinner like the rest of humanity. Respect is what each human being deserves and owes to the other. If, at the very worst, the act of homosexuality is seen as a sin, well, everyone is a sinner, and anyone born of a man and woman that denies being a sinner has committed an act of sin by such denial. To date, none alive can 'cast the first stone,' as we all sin in thought, word, and deed. Have you not heard that if anyone were to be judged based on their thought process, they would end up in prison? Have you not wondered why no one alive is ever recommended for sainthood? How can a sinner pass judgement or prescribe punishment for a fellow sinner? Let He or She who is without sin and is Holy be the judge and executor of punishment to sinners, as no human being is worthy or qualified to do such. Humanity needs to focus on crime and criminals and do no harm to self and/or others.

Black and White

It is critical to keep in mind that nothing will change until all the wrong concepts that make up the foundations upon which humanity builds are removed and replaced with human-friendly ones.

Foundations are critical to anything; as such, anything without foundation cannot stand. It is not a rocket science to know the concept of assignation of colour to unequal but equally important human beings is a design of man. Many would argue that it is a good thing for many reasons; however, it is the intended outcome that determines whether it is a good or bad thing. Every sane and objective human being knows that real colours as known and designed by man is not attributable to human beings but can be found in some animals.

In life, there are black, white, and brown horses, but irrespective of their different colours, they are, and remain, all equally horses. There is no division amongst horses based on their colours, and what a healthy black horse can do, a healthy white or brown horse will do likewise. Horses do not discriminate on the grounds of colour. There are also white, black, and white Goats that remain equally Goats too. But when it comes to human beings, unless one is deluded and wants to remain deluded, black and white are not applicable, because no human being is either white or black. If colour assignation to unequal but equally important human beings becomes necessary for whatsoever reason, it should only be on the grounds of colour most relative to the individual/s. It is certain that the colours most relevant to human beings are neither black nor white. Anyone who thinks otherwise does not only require a visit to a psychiatrist but an optician also.

In terms of colour relativity, it is very obvious that those classified as 'black' are closer to the colour brown and those classified as 'white' closer to yellow. The questions to ask are: 1) Whose idea was it to assign colours to human beings, and what exactly was their intention/s? 2) Why were these colours that are closer not considered, and if they were considered, not chosen?

Bearing in mind that every human being came into this world 'yesterday' very empty, vulnerable, and without concept, ideology, and theory, it is vivid that all human beings have done, based on observation of existing principles, is to copy, enhance, or minimise acts seen or heard. As a result, many continue to subscribe to a deadly, destructive and regressive concept such as the assignation of black and white colours to human beings. A concept born out of sheer wickedness by ill-informed and irrational fore-bearers who came into this world as weak and vulnerable as you and I, but one day something happened and the feeling of invincibility crept in, and grandiose thoughts came in. In this deluded mindset, an idea was suggested and could have easily been suggested over an alcoholic drink, tobacco, and illicit drug:

"Let us distinguish between good people and bad people by assigning the colour black to them and white to us. Let us ensure that everything bad is attributable to the colour black, including the selection of a Pope; so the black flame will represent negative, and white flame positive. This will certainly make a psychological impact on humanity and this which can be embedded into our children, for our posterity. We have to be crafty in how we sell the idea to the recipients."

It would not be surprising that whoever came up with the idea not only received a 'worthy round of applause' but also an award and honour from the highest office in the land, as many agreed with the proposal. The person who came up with the idea and those who bought the idea were not only to blame; the blame also goes to those who accepted it and those who saw nothing wrong with the concept.

However, what the person who came up with this idea and those who agreed and accepted it failed to realise was that a dangerous seed that was going to play a huge part in 'blinding' and 'amputating' humanity was sown. This weird idea contributed to the most naturally resourced continent of our world that ought to be the seat of production and manufacturing being turned into a consumer continent by both external and internal forces.

A continent such as Africa with at least half of the world's natural resources locked up and fictitiously designed only for exploitation by many at the helm of affairs inside and some countries outside of it. In doing so, some Africans and many outside of Africa have contributed, and continue to contribute, to the afflictions of humanity. It goes without saying that when a spade is wrongly given the name 'bread,' children may wish to eat it; hence a spade should be called a spade. This is not a 'them and us' affair but a collective affair, as our derailment owes not to any particular individual, community, or nation but to foundations laid before our arrival in this transient human life. The adverse effect of which has led to a broken world.

According to the novelist and author Chimamanda Adichie who addressed an audience in one of the TED TALKS regarding what she called "The danger of the singular story," or one-sided story, a singular story about an individual, community, country, or continent is not only incomplete and wrong but also false. She remembered growing up in a household with a living-in domestic help named 'Fide.' She told her listening audience, "The only thing my mother told us was that his family was very poor. My mother sent yams, rice, and our old clothes to his family, and when I didn't finish my dinner, my mother would say, 'Finish your food; don't you know people like Fide's family have nothing?' So I felt enormous pity for Fide's family." One Saturday they went to Fide's village for a visit and Fide's mother showed them a beautifully patterned basket made by Fide's brother. Chimamanda was 'startled,' as it hadn't occurred to her that anybody in Fide's family could make something useful and be productive. According to her, this was because "all I had heard about them was how poor they were so that it had become impossible for me to see them as anything else but poor. Poverty was my singular story of them."

She recalled her experience when she travelled to America, aged 19, for her university education. Her American roommate was shocked by her and asked where she learnt to speak English so well and was 'confused' when she said to her that English is the official language spoken in Nigeria. Her American roommate asked her if she could listen to what she called "my tribal music" and, according to Chimamanda, was "consequently very disappointed when I produced my tape of Mariah Carey." Chimamanda when on, "...what struck me was this: she had felt sorry for me even before she saw me. Her default position towards me as an African was a kind of patronising well-meaning pity. My roommate had a single story of Africa, a single story of catastrophe. In this single story, there was no possibility Africans being similar to her in anyway ...no possibility of a connection as human equals."

Just like Chimamanda had a singular story about Fide's family from her mother, so did her American roommate about Africa and Africans from either her parents, books she read, institutions she attended, media, and her particular network. This is relevant to each and every one of us. The question is: What is the one singular story we have told or received about an individual, religious group, community or nation? Singular stories are negative, poisonous and hazardous to humanity. The negative foundations laid before us has made humanity guilty of telling a dangerous singular story, especially of those different from us who have so much to offer not only themselves but us and the entire humanity.

The questions to consider in metaphoric sense are as follows: In a world designed as a human body, how possible is it that the body would survive or be healthy if the hand had a negative singular story about the leg or decides to call the leg bad and seeks to devalue and/or destroy the leg? Or, looking at the world from the 'Five Finger' theory perspective, what will happen to the hand if one or two of its fingers have a negative singular story about any of the fingers of the rest or cause them to malfunction?

It is important to know that what is happening to Africa and its people have put enormous pressure on humanity and the entire world beyond anyone's imagination and comprehension. Has any individual, community, or nation considered what would happen to the world's economy and employment when, and if, Africa (which is theoretically the world's largest economy in terms of natural resources) harnesses only 75% of its natural resources? It is important to appreciate that the perception and devalue of Africa and its people today owes a lot to the conception of Black and White as representing Good and Bad in human beings. This is not a physical but a psychological thing that drives what is seen in the physical. As such, no amount of plausible policies which preclude this concept which lies at the root of the malfunction seen in humanity will work, until humanity is brave and rational enough to uproot this irrational concept and replace it with the 'Five Finger' theory and principles.

It is my take that, in its quest to create good and bad as described above, humanity pursued colour assignation to human beings. It ignored all the colours closer to it such as brown and yellow because they are too neutral and unable to convey the intended ideas. Humanity needed colours that would define and embody good and bad; however, humanity forgot or ignored (in its confusion) the fact that bad and good have no colour. Humanity wrongly assumed that by assigning everything bad to those classified as black and anything good to those classified as white, bad and good would react in the same fashion. Humanity failed to appreciate that 'the leg and hand' are vital components of the body just like the differences it possesses. By this formulation, ill-thought out ideas emerged, which are wreaking havoc from both coveted and overt perspectives.

Those who think this does not matter are, and will remain, part of the problem. Anything made with negative intentions will produce negative intention. This may not matter to some or many, but this is a negative psychological seed sown that needs to be addressed objectively in humanity's quest to become rational. Bad thoughts produce wrong actions. A poisonous seed will grow into a poisonous tree which must bear poisonous fruits; irrespective of how one carries out a root and branch action, the tree will remain poisonous until it is uprooted and a positive seed planted.

Humanity needs to wake up to the fact that all the isms—be it sexism, fascism, and racism—stem from dangerous seeds planted by irrational ancestors who knew little about the constructs of life and the world they came to rent, not own. As a result of those seeds, different parts of the same body responsible for different functions for the benefit of all turned against themselves. Humanity needs to realise this and collectively challenge and root out all those aged and dangerous seeds causing it to malfunction. It is not for one gender, ethnicity, colour, creed, or nationality, but all to deal with.

TWO WARRING NATIONS OVER IDENTITY

Why do human beings fight for ownership of something or someone when it is good and seek to reject the same when it is bad? A rational mind will think and act differently. In as much as it is a fact that individuals are best suited to define their own identity, it cannot be right for one to define themselves as God or choose the colour red as the colour most reflective of their complexion, neither is it right for any country to impose identity on an individual for self-interest and own purpose. A definition has to be objective and incorporative of facts, and should not be made up depending 'on the weather of the day.'

A case in question is Anthony Joshua who became the IBF Heavyweight Champion of the world on 11th April 2016. Anthony is a young man whose parents are from Nigeria but has lived most of, if not all, his life in Britain. His nationality had not been an issue until he became a world heavyweight champion.

Some sections of Nigeria and British people have gone into a verbal war of claiming the champion to be their own. What is, however, not in doubt is that Nigeria and Britain can describe and define Anthony as they want, but the objective and real description that incorporates the facts is clear. Some Nigerians cited the fact that when a Nigerian, born in Britain, commits a crime, the British media refers to such individual as 'Nigerian-born,' but when a Nigerian, born in Britain, becomes a star or renowned celebrity like in the case of Anthony Joshua, the British media would say, 'The British Champion,' instead of 'Nigerian-Born Champion.' It is a shameful fact that Nigeria, as most African countries, is renowned for not being interested, let alone seeking out and investing in their talents, but when another nation or the individual rises to prominence, then Nigeria, as well as many other nations in Africa, becomes interested.

All these are parts of the irrational behaviours witnessed in human beings as a result of non-fulfilment of the three stages of nurturing required for a human being to become rational. In a metaphoric sense, these African countries and others across the globe act like an irresponsible parent who negates the needs of their principal assets (children) and has no interest in them as the waste. However, when another responsible parent with compassion sees to the needs of the irresponsible parents' children and enables them to reach or maximise their potential, then the irresponsible parent wakes up and begins to fight over the children they had thrown to the dogs.

Remembering the former American President Bill Clinton's speech when he visited Nigeria in 2000 and spoke about a Nigerian/American Inventor and Scientist (Philip Emeagwali) who he described as "One of the great minds of the information age." He told his listening audience that as he drove from the airport, he noticed that "there's another Philip Emeagwali," a hundred, or even a thousand Philip Emeagwali wasting on the streets of Nigeria today, who do not have the means to take their talents out. He stated:

"It is our responsibility' to ensure that those children harness their respective talents so, they (Nigerians) and the rest of the world do not miss the benefit of their contributions."

However, what may have been visible to Mr. Clinton were the many Emeagwalis he could see but those that were not obvious to him were many of those children who were killed in various ways, either through accidents of all sorts, malnutrition, curable illnesses, and fetish belief systems operational in Nigeria and many African countries. It was not only many Emeagwalis being wasted but many Imafidons who have been described in many reputable quarters as "The smartest family in Britain," Sandie Okoro who, in 2016, was appointed by World Bank Group as the Senior Vice President and General Counsel, and many Bennet Omalus who, in 2016, received the highest medical award in United States of America, to mention but a few.

The true identity of an individual is self-defined. A sensible child would lean towards the guardian who took care of them than a biological mother who did not give a damn whether they were dead or alive. However, no one should be denied or deny themselves of all the ingredients that made them who they became.

When one, as an individual, community, country, or continent, grows beyond shame, they start to exist, not live.

The Objective View

The truth is, without Nigeria, the world would not have known the man called Anthony Joshua, and without Britain, Anthony Joshua is likely not to have become the fighter he became. As such, the objective identity and definition is that Anthony Joshua is both and equally Nigerian and British. None of his heritage should be denied for whatever purpose, either by himself or someone else. Nigeria has a claim because without having parents who originate from Nigeria, Anthony Joshua, as we know and call him, would not have been. Having said that, Nigeria and indeed many African nations are renowned for not investing in their talents; therefore, it is very likely that Anthony Joshua would not have become the boxer he is now without being a part of the British establishment. It is a common saying that “he or she who pays the piper calls the tune.” However, it is wrong to strip someone of an integral part of them for any reason. In view of this, the objective position in good as in bad, in terms of the right identity, should be Nigerian/British or British/Nigerian. Anything left is for the individual to define themselves as they would prefer to be described.

If your name is not Ron, but I’ve grown so used to calling you Ron, how would you feel if I insist on calling you Ron because ‘I’m so used to it, I grew up calling and believing that your name is Ron, and it is so difficult for me to change now; it is convenient and would incur a lot of adjustments which will be very difficult for me?’

I have checked and can confirm that I am a human being like everyone currently living in this world but at the same time, I am different and enjoy the difference I bring to the equation. I do not wish or want to be someone else, because if I become someone else, one of us would become completely valueless and useless. The differences I see in myself are numerous and fascinating. But they are only useful when in partnership, collaboration, and complementary alliance with others. Some of these differences are subjective, objective, funny and realistic—for example, when others are watching their weight, I choose to watch my height; when others are either white or black, I realise that the colour most relevant to me is brown; and when others believe they are rational, I worked out that humanity has the capacity but has not reached the level required in order to become rational, hence there is severe malfunction in our world. It is also the difference in me that led me to take the unusual step of making my funeral oration an integral part of this book, to ensure there is no misrepresentation of me in my absence.

I am sure that you would agree with me that it just does not make sense to accept what I know I am not and what I know is part of the cancers eating us as members of this human family. I do not wish to be black, neither do I wish to be white, as those two colours have no relevance to the colour of my skin or anyone's skin. I never asked or chose to be any of these colours; therefore, I cannot subscribe to something that is alien to me. I do not want to be associated with any of the negative and/or positive connotations linked to these colours. All I know is that good and bad have no colour, but our ill-informed and irrational forebearers thought wrongly that they could design in human beings good and bad by colour assignation of everything bad is black, and everything good is white, including the selection of the Pope. Even though they got it all wrong, they still managed to sow the negative psychological seed. It is critical to know that both those who coined the idea and the recipients of the idea were at fault.

If I should or must have a colour more relevant to my skin type then, I know (not think) that the colour closest to my skin type is brown. I'm sure then that I AM A BROWN PERSON if that must be the case. I am happy to be linked with any negative and/or positive thing associated with being brown. Can you find any? Perhaps I am the one and only brown person on this planet we are all renting as tenants. Please do try and get used to calling me a 'brown man.'

I am one of the Ihenachos who was born in Ogwa, Imo State. I am an

Igbo man, a Nigerian, a British having lived more in Britain than I lived in Nigeria. I am from both continents of Africa and Europe. I am proud to have both heritage and delight in the blend of knowledge and exposure the two have given me. But above all, I am a citizen of the world, a full-fledged member of this human family and one human race with different parts. These are my entire heritage; none played more or less role in my life, but they were all equal contributors to the person I have become. These are my true heritage, which is undeniably factual. Until we can define ourselves and be sure of who we are, we will remain confused, owning things we do not know or things that have nothing to do with us. One will remain a stranger to even themselves, with strange concepts.

The Truth

The main reason why the truth is uncomfortable at times is that, irrespective of how one wants to bend, galvanise, or gloss over it, it remains unchangeable, unequivocal, and steadfast. Truths such as the nature of our tenancy here on earth and psychopathic nature of those who are not conscious of the truth ... the fact that there's only one human race with different parts that are each vital to this singular entity.

Remember that once it is objectively contestable, it cannot be the truth! The truth can only be subjectively and equivocally contested by devious and/or confused minds who either do not know what they are doing and/or deliberately want to confuse others for selfish and/or devious reasons. Hence they often ask, 'Whose truth?' For example, one plus one is two, and that's an unequivocal, unshakeable, irresistible and objective truth. Anyone contesting or challenging this truth can only do so on the platform of psychosis and/or psychopathy, because the truth has no imitation.

I have said it before, and I will continue to say, that our ancestors who laid those foundations were, if not less intelligent, obviously less exposed than us. Our world is broken today due to the dangerous concepts, ideologies, and theories laid by our ancestors who were afraid, believed in them and us and never saw the world as one entity, just like one human body with different parts for different actions in order for the body to be healthy and effective. A clever child does better and achieves more than their parents. A clever child will not insist on continuously plastering over cracked walls or building on dodgy foundation but would lay a solid foundation for a better house.

However, why must I tell you the truth, and why are you being encouraged to listen to the truth I profess? Quite simply, I am not one of the psychopathic or sociopathic politicians campaigning for votes, neither am I one of the devious preachers after your 10%. My main interest is in the fact that humanity is in trouble and this is the time to do something about it. But most importantly, I know that the truth is not only the way, but the truth is the only way. Darkness cannot stand in the face of light. The truth is too big and heavy; no one person, community, or nation can carry it. Therefore, each of us, as individuals, communities, and nations, has the some (not their own type of) truth. The truth is universal, standard and never confuses.

The same way horses are horses, irrespective of whether they are brown, white, or black, so are human beings, irrespective of their background, gender, age, status, colour (which obviously is neither white nor black), creed, or location. Humanity needs to feel sorry and ready to help those whose psychological deformity (from false information received from their ill-informed parents, guardians, institutions, peers, and society at large) has led to their struggle and the feeling of discomfort about this obvious truth.

The taste of the pudding is in the eating. It would have been surprising if we had a functional world when the theories, concepts, and ideologies that inform this life are faulty. The car being drivable does not necessarily mean the car is in a good working condition. The evidence of our living and chaos in our world proves that the theories that inform our lives and living are hopelessly wrong, faulty and false. These have exposed humanity to great danger. The time to save humanity is now. The theories, concepts, and ideologies that are responsible for this status quo are not only extremist but cancerous in nature. In dealing with it, moderation, fear, or silence will be futile, irresponsible and totally unproductive.

It is sinful, unethical, immoral and evil to use moderation or silence as a response to anything that seeks to damage any part of humanity which usually is extreme in nature. Such measure is as good as using a sleeping tablet for cancer treatment. Fear also cannot be used as a response to cancer; in fact, fear will hasten cancer's devastating impact on anyone. The best way to defeat cancer or buy more time is to confront and deal with cancer with the right form of treatment.

Mission Here On Earth

Every individual, community, and nation needs to do and should be encouraged to do whatever is necessary to harness all that's within it, be the best they can be, and bring together their peculiar and diverse attributes in partnership and in one accord with the spirit of exchange to make this one entity called the world a better, stronger and safer place for all.

The mission is for each individual, community, and nation to be the best they can be and maximise their respective potentials. Each should know that any agenda set to cheat, suppress, dominate, or devalue self and/ or another in any way, shape, or form on the premise of superiority or inferiority is psychopathic. Such agenda is wrong and delusional, and it is upon this type of agenda and platform that all manner of evils are conceived and engendered.

We are charged to be the best we can be, as individuals, communities, and nations, without thinking the worst of ourselves, any other, or others. As a part of this world, we are to ensure our interest at all cost, so long as it is not at the expense or detriment of any other or others. We should, at all times, think first what we can give before we think what we can get or take. Everyone, every community, and every nation has something to give, but if there is nothing to give, then there is nothing to take. Our mission here on earth is for each to see ourselves as representing a hand which can only become clean by washing the other hand, and the other hand washing it.

No Human Being Is Perfect

Every human being conceived in the conventional way by a male and female is not without flaws or immune from a mental disorder. As inspired as anyone is presently or in the past, there will always be a shortcoming in anything conceived by anyone born of a woman, no matter what they represent to humanity spiritually or politically. No one born in this way is God, Allah, or Jehovah. Therefore, in view of the diversities and the importance of differences in the survival and posterity of humanity, any doctrine, policy, or agenda based on or geared towards dominance, superiority, or inferiority linked to humanity is false, deluded and misconceived. The proponents and follower of such doctrines, policies, and agendas did not, and do not, understand what it is to be human beings. Such people were, and are, irrational, irrespective of their perceived wisdom, academic achievements, and material wealth.

Humanity needs to do whatever it takes to ensure that such malfunction and such foundations are either corrected or uprooted, as they serve as cancers dismantling and destined to ruin humanity. If anyone, irrespective of creed or political affiliation, does not understand that there would be nothing called tall if short did not exist, and no one will be able to recognise their religious persuasion if other religious groups did not exist, then the person is still emotionally immature, irrespective of age and social standing. Without the unbeliever, there will be no believer, and both are critical. There is no reason for one to become critical of the other. All that is required is mutual respect, exchange of views with a view to agree, disagree, or agree to disagree. When an agreement is reached to disagree, it serves no purpose to revisit the same issues unless there is new information to consider from either side. We, as human beings, are like fruits on top of the tree that will not ripe at the same time, and both the ripped and the un-ripped are important and valuable.

GENERATIONAL COMPONENTS TO DOMESTIC VIOLENCE

The pursuit of fairness and mutual respect is defeated if the agenda is to hold the oppressor/s in a rebound. No one can correct or achieve fairness with hatred on their mind; rather, they are likely to achieve 'the same traffic in the opposite direction'.

The quest for a better world also cannot be achieved by masking nor colluding with copy cats neither with inadequacies and mediocrity for whatever reason. The fact that 'it' happened to one does not mean it happened to all, and every case is different. Therefore, it is important not to join the 'bandwagon' on the grounds of gender, colour, or creed.

Every case should be treated on its own merit, and the law should cut on both sides. Cases should, and must, be pursued on an individual basis with a primary focus on justice, not for enhancement of statistics for political gains, the pursuit of promotion by law enforcement agencies, or other 'invisible' reasons damaging to humanity. One miscarriage of justice for whatever reason is one too many and a stain on humanity, especially when the evidence is clear from the onset to the contrary.

Blame and finger pointing between men and women, 'black' and 'white,' religious groups, different ethnicities, cultures, and nations are only an empowerment to the children of this world to continue on the path of self-destruction and mutilation. It is time—not only to look at each case on its deserving merit but time for adults to grow and own up, learn lessons and, even if theirs is a lost battle, ensure that the children learn from their parents' mistakes and right the wrongs of the past for posterity. People need to face up to their mistakes and ensure that they not only learn from them but that their children learn, so they do not go on to repeat them.

According to Toniaamaka Chrisokere, "If last generation considered this generation, we would not have been in this mess we are in now." Repeating the same old mistakes will produce the same or worse outcomes, being that change is inevitable. Is there any difference between an infant and adult who says "Look at that young boy; does he look like a bad boy?" or thinks that his or her father is the strongest or wisest man on earth?

If a child can say to one of their parents, "You are to blame for my failure, because when I was one-year-old, you called me a bad name," it is obvious that the other parent said something to the child. The question is, even if (though highly unlikely) it is true that such thing was said to a one-year-old, what could be the purpose of anyone, let alone a parent, telling a child this? Who else could be present when a child is one year old to say something of this nature to a child?

One does not need to consult with empirical and statistical evidence to know that domestic violence is at the root of violence of all kinds, including wars and terrorism in our world. The said violence is one of the awful cancers gripping humanity. Men are the main perpetrators of domestic violence, whilst women are the primary victims according to statistics. Statistics also have it that in England and Wales, on average, two women are killed every week through domestic violence. The reasons for this is clear, because men are generally physically stronger than women. Hence the law must insist that wherever and whenever a woman calls for help, the law should respond, and respond quickly, without delay.

It is also important (though not easy in most cases) that victims appreciate that violence is not part of any human relationship, let alone a loving relationship. Anyone who can attack someone once is very likely to do it again. During the violence anything can happen, including permanent damage or death, when they attack again. Therefore I enjoin that people should choose life, which is the basis for everything, than remain in such a relationship. Having said that, it is of vital importance to appreciate that within this generalised rule of men being the main perpetrators of domestic violence lies significant exceptions. The exceptions being that some men are going through hell at the hands of violent women who do not only abuse them physically but emotionally too, especially in the United Kingdom and the United States where rightly genuine attempts (though still not adequate in view of statistical evidence) have been made to protect the interest of women.

According to Mankind Initiative, "13.2% of men state they have been a victim of domestic abuse since they were 16 (27.1% women). For every three victims of domestic abuse, two will be female, one will be male. These figures are the equivalent of 2.2 million male victims and 4.5 million female victims. One in four women and one in six men suffer from domestic abuse in their lifetime." From these statistics, it is likely that the reasons why fewer men die through domestic violence compared to women is the fact that men are more able to physically protect and defend themselves.

As in the case below, the man in question was able to duck objects thrown at him, run away, impound sticks, belt, and other objects aimed at him by the woman. However, he was unable to avoid the spitting, biting, hitting, and kicking. He was also unable to avoid water poured at him and ripped clothes, chains, and wrist watches. He also protected himself by barricading himself in his room whilst asleep each time he felt in danger. Men who suffer domestic violence suffer greatly due to shame, and even where one overcomes the shame, law enforcement agencies do either not take them seriously or are even slower to act compared to the way they act in women's cases. In view of this, it is fair to say that the system is letting both men and women down greatly.

On balance, it cannot be over-emphasised, and indeed it is only right, and proper to protect and defend the interest of women in domestic violence in view of the physical strength of men. It is also important because protecting the interest of women means protecting the interest of children as well in most cases. Having said that, it is a well-known fact that no matter how good a system is, it is open to abuse. Hence some women have abused and continue to abuse the system, whilst many others still continue to suffer domestic abuse and violence. In the end, those who abuse the system by being violent and feigning violated demean those who are genuine survivors of domestic violence. They also make a mockery of all the hard working organisations fighting this cancer that is tearing humanity apart. The key thing to appreciate by those who see violence as a response to disagreements is, there is always an alternative, so long as violence has not commenced.

Violence always makes any situation worse; it is never a part of any relationship and should not be acceptable in any language, culture, or tradition. Any response to a violent act cannot be classified as violent, so long as it is proportionate and within reason; after all, the first rule in this singular 'life without duplicate' is 'self-defence and self-preservation.'

For society to move in the right direction towards dealing with this cancer, it needs not be a game of 'them and us.' Therefore, every right-minded man, including those who have suffered domestic abuse, needs to join hands with all those fighting against domestic violence towards women and vice versa. In the case of the man below, it was primarily women who knew what he had been going through, who saw him come into work sometimes in wet and torn clothes, human bites, and in distress that gave him support and encouragement. Men and women desperately need each other for complementary, collaborative and partnership purposes, as no gender can exist let alone survive on its own. We must learn to appreciate and respect what each gender brings to the table.

It is of critical importance to state that whilst it is important to investigate, prosecute, and severely punish perpetrators of domestic violence, it is also critical not to bring assumptions based on stereotype into the equation. After all, only an insane father wants his daughter to be a victim of domestic violence and insane mother wants her son to suffer the same fate or wants her son's partner to destroy him based on malicious, fabricated and devious lies as a result of hatred, especially if her son is the victim of the alleged domestic violence. A sane mother will be aggrieved if her son had sought help and support but (just like many women) got let down by the law enforcement agencies who end up, through their actions, empowering and joining the female perpetrator to falsify evidence in court against her innocent son in order to boost statistics, achieve promotion, or for whatever hidden agenda there is.

Hidden Background to Domestic Abuse

When children from an early age are misled to think or believe that violence is a means of 'resolving conflict,' forcing through a selfish and greedy agenda no matter how ill thought out, winning a lost argument by false and/or forced imposition of will in order to stay in control or through intimidation as means of keeping hold of what is not theirs; they copy, replicate, reduce, or enhance the behaviour. For example, when a father whose glorifying tribute to his late wife in the presence of his daughter and son-in-law reads, "My late wife was a powerful woman," and the qualification for his late wife being a 'powerful woman' was, "When I was being conferred with a chieftaincy title, all the women in our family were charged with the responsibility of cooking the food for the ceremony. However, one of the women refused to help in preparing and cooking the food. When the food was ready, the woman who refused to help came to take some food, and my late wife smashed a stick on her head." What does anyone expect the daughter to learn from such glorification of violence? This father (supported by his daughter) became angry and accused the son-in-law of disrespecting him because the son-in-law stated that it was not good to glorify violence. This man, in every story to do with his late wife, revolved around "My wife was a powerful woman"; he would lie, "She was a Major in the Army," even though she was an Auxillary Nurse in the Army. He would always qualify his statement by citing an event where she either threatened to slap someone, slapped, or beat someone up.

The same father witnessed his daughter in an argument with her husband inside the house. His daughter was wearing her night dress whilst carrying a flower verse; she began to hit the flower verse on her husband's car, screaming and calling her husband to come outside for a fight. The father remained inside and said nothing. On the day her father was to travel back to his home country from England, her husband, whilst giving him a lift to the airport, brought up that incident as the father-in-law was giving him advice on 'how to use wisdom in marriage.' The son-in-law asked him what his thoughts were about what his daughter did on that day she was outside attacking the car and inviting him out for a fight. The son-in-law was dumbfounded when his father-in-law replied, “You were very lucky that day, I have to be honest with you. If I were her, I would have set that car on fire.” The son-in-law who usually would hang about at the airport until his father-in-law checks in was so shocked at hearing this he never said another word, and had to drop him off and left.

This same father-in-law, in one of his advice sessions on how to live in peace as husband and wife, told his son-in-law in the presence of his daughter, “A man has to be tolerant. A real man can take anything from his wife. Even a former Governor of Imo State in Nigeria was slapped by his wife, and as a man, he took it and simply walked away.” At that point, the son-in-law reminded him that he was not prepared to hear any stories about violent people and violent relationships. His son-in-law asked him how many times his current wife has slapped him, but got no response. The father-in-law and his daughter felt insulted. However, having forgotten about giving this advice, one day, the same man went to visit his son who then lived in the Southeast of London.

When he returned, he said to his son-in-law, “My son is suffering at the hands of that woman he is living with. You know, as a man, there are things a woman will do, and you just feel like giving her a good kick.” As he was saying this, he was demonstrating the kick with his right leg. The son-in-law then asked him, “I thought you told me that the mark of a man is a man who can take anything from his wife?” His father-in-law remembered what he said, went into his shell in ‘momentary shame and embarrassment.’ The son-in-law also reminded him that he was aware of his son’s violence towards his wife. He was told that his son’s wife had come at least once with a black eye covered with sunglasses as a result of an object thrown at her by his son. In addition, his son’s wife also said that on one occasion, his son, in anger, lifted her up and threw her on top of their newborn baby.

This father-in-law, without shame, had slang referring to himself as a little child who does not mind who is going out with his mother so long as his two hands are full of chicken legs: “Onye osoro ya kporo nnem, ihem nma wu ya kpawam ukwu okuko n’akam abua.” He also has stated on numerous occasions (when advised by his son-in-law that people should work hard to earn their living) that "some people are born to take risks."

On a separate occasion, the same father-in-law, in expressing his 'special love' for his other daughter with whom he ran into conflict, said, in the presence of his son-in-law, two of his daughters, and one of his sons, "This is my daughter I love so much. To prove the love I have for her, I used to give her the cane to flog her older sister sitting here if she got something wrong or misbehaved when they were small." This is an information the son-in-law has heard from his wife but had to ignore as it happened in the past (even though he did not find it funny), but to have it confirmed by the man who was behind such madness, let alone confirmed as an expression of love of one child over another, had to be welcomed with a frown at the very least. The son-in-law whose wife had to listen to this asked, "Chief (as he called him), did you?" His father-in-law became upset and shouted, "It is not your business. That is how I brought up my own children. You will do worse!" He (the father-in-law) went on and said all manner of things to his son-in-law and warned, "Don't forget you are only an in-law." He had become very aggrieved about his son-in-law because his son-in-law, on numerous occasions, had not agreed to his occultist ideologies geared towards extracting money using devious ways. One of those occasions was in 2005, following the burial of his son-in-law's mother.

Having seen that his son-in-law had become an orphan, he took a 'prophet' without consulting anyone and went to his son-in-law's compound because he 'loved' him so much and wanted, 'as a father, to protect him and all his belongings.' He claimed that they went on a mission to purify the compound, and as they were going, they saw a lady who was 'white' trying to flag them down. The said 'prophet' recognised that woman as evil and instructed that she should be ignored. When they got to the son-in-law's compound and began to pray, a 'big snake' came out, and on their way back, they saw the same woman and ignored her. He said that the prophet does not charge anything and all he spent was 45,000 naira to buy 'a few things, including a special candle.' He then said that the 'prophet' told him that one more visit to the compound was crucial and the list of things to buy for that important second visit was going to cost 90,000 naira.

His son-in-law diplomatically thanked him for what he said he did out of love. He, however, reminded his father-in-law that he was once a seminarian. He told his father-in-law that it would have been nice if he had informed him before embarking on such journey on his behalf. He informed his father-in-law that anyone who requires or demands anything before they prayed or did anything in the name of God is a fake. He reminded him that Jesus Christ and His disciples never asked for anything before they cast out demons or healed anyone. He also directed his father-in-law to read 2nd Kings Chapter 5 and see for himself that Elisha refused all the gifts presented to him by Naaman, the Commander of the Army of King of Aram whose leprosy was cured having followed the instruction of Elisha. He also asked him to read on and find what happened to Gehazi (servant of Elisha who ran after Naaman to falsely collect those gifts).

He finally reminded his father-in-law of what Christ said in Matthew 10 verse 8: "Heal the sick, raise the dead, cleanse those who have leprosy, drive out demons. Freely you have received, freely give." His father-in-law became angry, stating, "I am not a child. I am trying to safeguard your interest, and you are telling me stories." The father-in-law felt insulted and told his daughter that her husband was an ungrateful man who does not respect old age.

Things, however, took a turn for the worst in 2007. Prior to 2007, the second son and last child to this father-in-law was diagnosed as suffering from a Drug Induced Psychosis and his son-in-law, having a background in mental health, advised the entire family that the young man would need to be on anti-psychotic medication for a long while in order to control his symptoms and sustain a stable mental state.

In December 2006, the young man went on holiday and visited his father who secretly advised him to stop all his anti-psychotic medications and gave him olive oil to use instead. His son returned to England in January 2007, whilst his father came on holiday to England soon afterward. Throughout his stay in London between January and end of May 2007, the father never asked to be taken to go and see his ill son, especially having stopped him from taking his anti-psychotic medications, let alone go and see how he was getting on. He never went or asked to be taken to see his ill son who lived outside of London because there was no financial gain.

Soon after his departure, his son stabbed a window cleaner and killed one of the police officers who came to deal with the initial stabbing. News from BBC revealed that, in court, the young man revealed that he stopped his prescribed medication on the advice of his father—who replaced it with olive oil. This was how his son-in-law found out what transpired between him and his son. The son-in-law became greatly upset at the level of carelessness and stupidity of his father-in-law, considering the fact that he stopped his son from taking the desired treatment and did not have the sense to go and see how his son was doing without his anti-psychotic medication. The son-in-law felt that the stabbing of a window cleaner and killing of a police officer plus all the emotional torture and torment for the two-year-old, young wife, parents, and siblings of the dead police officer would have been prevented.

The height of his son-in-law's annoyance and frustration came when this father went about telling everyone that his son committed murder because "bad people, through black magic, made him to do it." His son-in-law told him not to create enemies by saying things that are unfounded. He (the son-in-law) pointed at the fact that his son stated in court that he stopped his prescribed medication for olive oil which (if not responsible) contributed to his relapse. This father became upset at hearing this but then, instead of feeling a sense of remorse, went as far as convincing his daughter, "The policeman who was killed was destined to die; it was just unfortunate that it was my son who killed him." Her daughter also jovially said to the husband at one point that one of her friends made the same statement that the policeman was destined to die, but it was unfortunate that it was her brother who killed him.

Nothing his son-in-law said or did could make this father-in-law think rationally. He later committed the worst atrocity by instigating his daughter to explore ways to see if they can sue the Local Authority responsible for the care and treatment of his son for negligence. All these made the son-in-law weary, and because he criticised these inhumane and senseless thought process, this father then convinced his daughter that it was her husband that led her brother (his son) to kill a policeman. The son-in-law was declared as the number one enemy to this father and his household. This man and his entire household believed that they are responsible for everything good in their life, but anything bad that happens to them, someone else is responsible. Their belief system which they mix with Christianity was too weird to understand for the man's son-in-law.

In the same year 2007, the first son of this same father also was sent to prison for another unrelated crime. These two incidents in one year brought untold chaos, and the man's daughter began to stay out of her marital home more than usual. Every attempt made by her husband to see how best to support her was turned into an argument and/or violence. The combination of pressure from her father to destroy her marriage and the imprisonment of her two brothers in the same year was too much to bear. Her husband was able to see these, but every suggestion for her to seek help was interpreted as "You are saying that my family are mad." She went as far as sending a text message to her husband's relatives, asking them to warn him that she would "pull him down" if he did not take care.

Her father continued to visit but clearly with the intention to see to the end of that marriage. He would bring his daughter 'special prayer book' where incarnation of all sorts, including placing a curse on someone and praying for a marital breakthrough in the name of Jesus, is obtainable. He encouraged his daughter to start living her own life and doing her own things. He even told his daughter never to sleep with a husband that disrespects him, the father-in-law. However, in 2011, as this father was going to turn 70 with none of his other children anywhere to be found, he used his craft to extract £500 in cash from his daughter and son-in-law.

His son-in-law ended up paying for flight tickets and expenditure for himself and his wife who were the only direct family members in diaspora present at the event. For the sake of the children, his son-in-law had to succumb to the blackmail, because they had planned to wreck everything if his daughter did not attend, even though his 'special' daughter and his two sons were guaranteed to be absent. Even though the man's first son had relocated to Nigeria, he did not attend his father's 70th birthday celebrations. However, this gesture from his son-in-law was still not going to save the marriage. The son-in-law had overheard his father-in-law advising his wife:

"Ada mu (meaning, my first daughter), a husband can go anytime; first daughters and their fathers are one. You are my beloved daughter. In my previous life, you were my wife; that's why there is nothing I cannot do for you. I have to tell you that if your husband insults me or any member of our family, I will support you in any action you take. If he says anything about our family, you are within your right to do anything. Your husband does not respect old age. He has no respect for me. No marriage is for life. I want you to know that whatever you decide to do, I will support you. I don't think he is your real husband; I know you made a mistake and one man of god has revealed that to me. Husbands will come, and husbands will go, but I will remain your father. You can see that he does not like anything about you. He drove your brother out, and look what happened. If your brother were living with you, what happened would not have happened. Your husband does not know that England is for women, and whatever a woman says is what must be done."

When his son-in-law asked him why he was saying these, he denied it all and claimed that he was advising his daughter on how to live in peace with him. Following this, his daughter would find any excuse to leave the bedroom she shared with her husband and proceed upstairs where her father stayed, though she slept in a separate bedroom. Her father seemed to enjoy the fact that only him can his daughter listen to.

The son-in-law tried to talk to some older people in their community, but a combination of the father-in-law being untruthful by suggesting that he was all for peace and the fact that many in his community chose to be on the side of both wrong and right in spirit of not offending anyone, and enjoying silently seeing other families broken apart, as it offers them easy access and feeds the gossip culture, coupled with the fact that it offers them consolation that their own homes are not too badly broken, hampered any progress. This is a community where, in general (though there are exceptions), what people present as united families outside is totally different from what is going on inside. Everyone is busy telling the other person what they want to hear; no one seems to know what is right or wrong anymore, and the most advice one gets is: "Hapu ihe ahu"—meaning "leave that thing."

The son-in-law began to witness odd behaviours, ranging from his wife disappearing from their home for days to violent acts towards him. She went as far as beating up her mother-in-law, slapping her husband's auntie, involving herself in a physical altercation that led to the damage of a child's necklace in church and having to be suspended from work for threatening to slap a colleague. Those behaviours she grew up seeing from her parents and being celebrated and glorified by her father. Police were called, at least three times, on occasions where her behaviour was not only a threat to the health and safety of her husband but her children.

On one particular occasion, she pulled down the plasma television and was breaking all the framed pictures with glasses flying everywhere. The police witnessed all the broken glasses, and the television crashed face down on the ground, but she cleverly took the female officer into the kitchen, saying, "I am emotionally and psychologically abused." In the end, the police left with these words: "If we are called out again, we will start arresting people." The female officer gave her information about victim support, and from then, she believed she was a victim.

The incident that triggered a major change towards the collapse of the union occurred in 2011, as the woman in question was about to celebrate her 40th birthday. Within this period, the husband's brother-in-law was around as he was in transit and on Friday before her birthday the following Tuesday, she told her husband from her workplace that she would not be coming home and wanted "to cool off." She stated that she had already informed their visitor. She did not return until late on her 40th birthday.

Following her return, she relocated her bedroom on the second floor. Her husband decided not to say anything, to see if she was going to say something, until after two weeks. When she was asked what was going on and where she went to celebrate her birthday, she replied, "I will never tell you." Her husband told her that even though he never subscribes to a third party marriage, he would have to tell people for the first time, being that what had happened was threatening the foundations of the union. She told her husband, "If you want, go and bring Obama; I will never tell you." The husband left the issue for a while and later asked again, and this time, got:

"I went to cool off in a hotel on my own. I can show you details of where I went on the condition that you go and mend fences with your eldest sister and her husband." Her husband told her that the relationship of her sister and husband does not depend on whatever is happening elsewhere; therefore, there was no basis for their own relationship to depend on what is happening between him (the husband) and his sister. She then insisted that she would never say or show details of where she celebrated her 40th birthday. On the third time of asking, she then said, "I went out with my CEO, and we plan to have a child together."

At that point, the husband made it clear that he would inform some members of their community. In spite of all said and done, she still insisted on not saying anything. Whilst this was going on, her father sent a text message from abroad, claiming to be a relative of the husband living in America and abusing the husband:

"... u are a big foll iam one of ihxxxxxos fam frm usa we are tired of ur ltrs u are a disgrs to our fam. Uare un to mng ur fam what a shame. Luk nobds wife is an angel. It is only wit wisdom nd love dat fam goes on. If u miss dis ur wife who chldrn fr u my bro u are gone i tell u di trut. Go nd appease di land of ekwerazu fr what u did nd be free. Stop disturbing us in usa we are tired of u. U are empty indeed. Authur my foot indeed. Ur wife has seen shit. Poor lady.Ann Anyaegbu0806OXXXXXX."

The husband, knowing his father-in-law and the way he writes, knew he sent this text, as he thought that he had informed his relatives in America. Efforts from those informed by the husband brought some form of resolution but still did not get her to say where she went.

She insisted on meeting people separately where she can tell all sorts of lies, cry for sympathy and get away with what she wanted. She preferred situations where nothing she said could be contested or verified. She was feeling vindicated and feeling the support she was getting from all corners. She began to do as she pleased to the extent that her long-standing nasal operation date came, she decided not to let her husband know. Her husband, on remembering the hospital appointment, looked for her, as she was about to go into the theatre, but she left a standing order that no information should be given to him. Her husband, later on the same day, took all the children to go and see her; she refused the husband from coming in to see her.

On the day of discharge, she yet again refused to be picked up by her husband and, instead, was collected by a friend of their family where she stayed for five days. The husband to her friend who was also friendly with her husband and one of those her husband complained to about her behaviour had the cheek to tell her husband, "Your wife told us that the two of you are divorced. You even told us that you have had enough. There is nothing wrong in her staying here to recover from her operation. Other people had come and stayed with us following an operation in hospital." She stayed there for a week before returning to her home. At the end of all these, her husband travelled to her hometown to see her father and people in search of a resolution. It ended up that her father hid in his room and refused to see his son-in-law. This, her husband found as an unusual behaviour (being that her father was not responding to her husband, which got her husband worried, especially as his maids said that he was in his room).

Her husband then called the police (as in that part of the world, Ambulance Service is only for the dead) to carry out a welfare check, as he became worried that his father-in-law may have suffered a heart attack. Having overheard his son-in-law calling the police, he must have sent a text message to his new wife, informing her of what was happening. This resulted in the simultaneous arrival of his wife and the police officers. It was clear that she had been summoned home, as the anxiety others were expressing about her husband, she did not have; rather, she was asking why the police were called. She appeared very relaxed and even offered the police officer's seat before going inside to talk to her husband.

In the end, they both came out claiming that the father-in-law had been sick. The self-acclaimed sick man later labelled his son-in-law's action as anything but humane and claimed that his son-in-law brought "thugs" with "**dangerous weapons like digger and other dangerous and offensive weapons**," which is outrageous. The behaviour of the father-in-law and his new wife, whose pre-requisite for marrying him was that his children would take her as their mother, led the son-in-law to travel to his father-in-law's village to lay a complaint and made it clear that he had gotten fed up of the entire union. Prior to his arrival back to Britain, his father-in-law had informed his wife that he was attacked by her husband and thugs.

On his return, the man was warned by his wife to expect the unexpected as it was her turn. Her disappearance from home increased, and everything turned into an argument culminating in her instructing her daughter to call the police for her husband in 2011. On the day of the incident, her husband came back in the evening as she was speaking to the children, and as soon as she saw her husband, she began to use swear words. Her husband told her to stop using foul language in front of the children, and she quickly removed her footwear and in anger threw it at her husband and gave him a chase. Her husband ran into the kitchen, which was opposite the living room where she was sitting and tried to use the door to prevent her from coming in to attack him. She kept pushing and then asked their daughter to call the police.

The police arrived, and as she struggled to say why she called them, she pointed at whatever injury she had on her foot (whether she sustained the injury as she was pushing the door, nobody knew). She said that her husband caused her the injury. The police immediately arrested her husband. Her husband was bailed and warned not to contact her, but she began to approach people, including a Reverend Father she had never met but only came to know because her husband told her about him. She began to solicit for a way out but wanted everything to work in her own terms. In the end, she withdrew the case, and because her husband was family orientated, he agreed to go back, primarily for the sake of the children.

Things began to get back to normal to the extent that in 2013, they had another child. The pregnancy surprised both parents. However, the person most upset about the reconciliation was the father of the wife who came into the country in early 2014 and was staying in another accommodation arranged by his daughter. He refused to see his son-in-law but was visiting his daughter in the absence of her husband. Every attempt made by his son-in-law to see her father was declined. However, on 30th April 2014, the son-in-law took time off in lieu, and as he was parking his car in the driveway, he noticed someone running from the back door into the garden. He went straight to the back garden and saw a scene he never wanted to see in his lifetime again. He saw an old man (his father-in-law) cowering like a naughty schoolboy. He felt so sad at seeing his father-in-law in a state like that and invited him inside but he, in his shame, remained in the garden.

When his son-in-law went inside the house to unlock the back door, which was locked by his wife in the pretence that no one ran outside, he saw the wife who pretended to be tidying up. He asked her, "Why is Chief outside?" and she replied, with a firm face, "Which Chief?" She then ran outside and instructed her father to go and wait for her at the library.

The husband made more attempts to meet up with the father-in-law but to no avail. Then it became obvious to the husband that they were planning on how to get rid of him. As soon as the father-in-law left the country towards the end of 2015, the plan to get rid of the husband began in earnest. It was one attack after another, and every little thing was turned into an argument.

The leaving and coming back without information increased, and physical attacks in front of the children intensified; 'call the police, call the police' became the song. However, the children were reluctant this time to call the police, and the man had no faith in what the police would do, having tried three times and was not able to even get the police to calm his wife down; rather, she was gradually made to feel a victim and made to feel she was above the law.

In December 2015, the man, having bought a lot of clothes for his wife and given the children their presents, had to listen to his wife ask the children what presents their friends got for Christmas. Her daughter told her that her friend, whose parents were divorced, travelled abroad to see her father and had an iPhone 6. This was met with "That is the benefit of divorce," as proclaimed by a mother to all her children. The man listened to this and was speechless in disbelief that a mother can say something as weird as this to her children. She began to do some weird prayers at night, using the prayer book supplied by her father who had told her that the person she was living with was not her real husband. Some parts of the prayer book read, "Let the angels of the living God roll away the stone blocking my marital breakthrough, in the name of Jesus." She followed this with persistent physical attacks at any given opportunity on her husband, perhaps the person she saw as the stone blocking her marital breakthrough.

Her husband, in the end, made up his mind to leave and informed their children, as he could no longer carry on living under threats of violence. On 16th January 2015, the unexpected happened as the man returned home around lunchtime to pick up his phone which he forgot, without knowing that his wife did not go to work. He never knew, because they were not communicating. On that day, the man was attacked by his wife, who told him, "Today is the day; you must leave this house." In the end, the man left and went back to work and decided not to return back to the house. He had to go, for the first time, with his relatives to take some of his belongings the following day. At that point, his wife knew that this was serious, because all along, the man has never involved his family members living in England in any of their disagreements. On 19th January 2015, his wife decided (certainly having liaised with her father) to cook up lies and accused her husband of domestic violence.

The husband was invited to the police station on 20th January and was arrested. He made it clear from the onset that he was the victim of domestic violence. He was bailed not to return to his home without a police escort. However, one day the husband contacted the police to assist him to return to his residence to collect some of his belongings, the police told him that they had limited *'man' power** and advised him to go either with a family member or friend. The husband went with a family member.

On arrival, his wife accused him of taking her unawares but did not make too much force to it. When the little baby saw his father, he ran towards him, but his mother rushed and took him back. The husband had noticed, prior to his arrival, that people were receiving inbox messages of unsavoury nature on Facebook and wanted to check whether it was coming from his home. He noticed that the lead connecting the Apple Mac to the socket had been removed. He decided to use the lead in the older computer in the kitchen. As soon as his wife realised what he wanted to do, she said to a family member, "No, I have to call the police. I was not told that he was coming here." She contacted the police and accused the husband of violating his bail condition. The husband checked the computer and found that she had broken into his Facebook account and was sending those messages. He quickly changed his password and turned off the computer. He remained silent and never said a word to his wife who was pacing about in a rage.

When the police arrived, they spoke to the husband and checked with their controllers, who confirmed that the husband had not broken his bail condition. They, however, said that the advice was for the husband to send a friend or family member. Whilst the husband was upstairs collecting some of his things, his wife was downstairs talking to some of the officers. Later, one of the officers she was talking to downstairs came up to the husband and said, "Your wife is saying that she feels unsafe with you having the keys, and is threatening to change all the locks. To prevent her from doing so, I advise you to give us your keys, and we will keep them safe in our station. Whenever you want to come next, we will make the keys available to you." The husband agreed to the advice and gave the police the keys on trust without knowing that the police officer handed the keys to the wife.

The husband wishes it noted that he had worked with and met many brilliant police officers in his life but sadly has seen a few that drag such an honourable service into the mud. He felt like the police officers involved in his case had already taken sides and were desperate to have him convicted at all costs. The police were acting as though it was a foregone conclusion that he would be found guilty at the Magistrates court. He felt that the police officers involved were not concerned with upholding the law or seeing that justice is served but were more interested in statistics, promotion, and other possible hidden agendas.

The husband got to know that the police officer had lied when he wanted to go back for more of his belongings. He agreed time with the police and went to his local police station to request the key. He was told by the officer manning the station, after inquiring, that it is quite usual for such arrangement to be made. The officer confirmed that the keys were handed over to his wife. When the man got to the house with the police, he found that all his belongings had been packed and moved from his room. When he eventually moved all his things, he noticed that he could not find hundreds of Dollars, Euros, expensive wristwatches, and many of his property.

On another occasion, the husband came to see his daughter, whom he had paid for to travel with her peers to visit NASA in Florida as part of her education, to finalise arrangements in terms of other things she may require for the trip. His daughter came out with her youngest sibling, and they all sat in the car. Suddenly, out of nowhere came his wife who double parked as though the husband was trying to run away with the children. Seeing how furious she was, the husband pressed the central lock as she charged pulling the doors and banging on the car. She pulled her mobile phone and called the police claiming that the husband had come to 'kidnap' the children. Soon afterward, an unmarked police vehicle turned up. One was talking to the wife and went to husband, and the other spoke to the daughter. Whilst the interrogation was going on, the little boy who saw his mother wanted to go to her and the father, realising this, wanted to release the child to run to his mother but the mother shouted, "You keep him there until the police finish with you." It took the police officer to tell her that it was okay for her son to come to her. The police did not see any kidnapping taking place and allowed the husband to go.

On the day of the court hearing, the wife, who was the perpetrator of violence, elected to have the screen pretending and mimicking genuine domestic abuse victims. She presented fabricated stories, including how the husband pushed her and she fell from two flights of staircase down.

She had to be reminded that there was a landing before the other set of staircase. She also brought as part of her evidence a damaged wall which she claimed was caused by her head as her husband smashed her head against the wall. There was no picture of the head that caused the damage, no treatment received, and the husband queried how "an egg can damage the wall and remain intact."

Furthermore, she even admitted that she became physically violent towards her husband first, as a defence to his verbal aggression. The husband informed the Magistrates of the let-down he suffered at the hands of Police whom he had called on three separate occasions and gave up, as they ended up making her believe she was above the law.

The police came and lied in court that they could only trace one call and that the husband only called them to report that his wife had mental illness. The husband, being a mental health professional, refuted the police statement by informing the bench that the police are no mental health workers to be summoned to deal with a mental disorder. With the combination of his wife's fabrications and police lies, the man was found guilty and not only made to do community service but asked to pay costs (though these were halted following the outcome of the appeal). The case was overturned in the Crown Court on appeal, where the wife came with more dramatic stories fit for the movies.

However, prior to the appeal hearing and boosted by her perceived victory in the Magistrates Court assisted by the Police and the Crown Prosecution Service, the wife decided to pursue a non-molestation order, injunction and sole ownership of their joint tenancy through the civil court. Her husband contested it, and the Judge felt that her story needed supporting evidence and adjourned the case pending her supporting evidence. She sought this evidence at all costs, and her father provided some supporting evidence, which included a statement he obtained from Nigerian Police Force—see below.

Her father, after doing this, arrived in the country with his new wife (as his daughter's biological mother is deceased) to support and push through his agenda to finally get rid of her husband. Her father's statement highlighted everything the man had said about his negative role not only in his daughter's marriage but all his children, especially the one that murdered a policeman. The statement read:

"THREATENED LIFE BY VIOLENCE: To day being 7-2-2012 at about 1220hours, One 'he mentioned his name' of Road 19 Federal Housing Estate Umuguma. Came to the station and reported that 4/2/2012 at about 0800 hours in the morning, one 'he mentioned his son in-law's name' M of 'he mentioned his son in-law's address in London' being his son inlaw came to his house with some unknown men numbering about five in numbers with some dangerous weapons like digger and other dangerous and offensive weapons. Complainant stated further that the said man has been threatening the whole family including his daughter 'he mentioned his daughter's name' been his wife even in London. He added that he was staying with them in the above mentioned address that he drove him out from his house in London and his violent nature made him to return back to Nigeria because he had no place to stay there that was the reason he came back to Nigeria pending when his daughter would find another accommodation there for him to return to Britain. Hence his report. Action: Entry was made for record purpose.W/CPL Obiajunwa Ijeome."

This statement had the Nigerian Police Force stamp, which was signed. It stated that it came from 'Federal Housing Police Station' and the name of the Assistant Superintendent of Police was mentioned therein. The statement is dated 7th February 2012 and time at 1220 hours. No doubt, money exchanged hands before he obtained such falsified document. This is the same man who tells the rest of the world that all he wants is peace and asks, "Am I going to marry my daughter?" The truth is that this man is not on his own, as many marriage break-ups in the Nigerian community, particularly Igbo community, stem from parents living in Nigeria or visiting their children abroad.

These parents are in various competitions in their local town meetings, religious gatherings, and the sustenance of these competitions has to be funded by their children abroad. It is the case that whenever they are not getting as much as they expect from their children abroad, their partners are seen as the obstacle. It is also a fact that when parents have made themselves very vulnerable to the fact that their livelihood is being sponsored by their children abroad, whatever those children say they want to do will automatically be supported by such parents. Parents who, in the past, used to support their children's marriages and ensure they are intact are now so dependent that they are easily bought over by their children, hence when their children say they want to do away with the man or woman in their lives, irrespective of the consequences on their grandchildren and wider community, they support wholeheartedly.

In this particular instance, this father was acting like a psychopath who was only after his own comfort and did not give a damn about the implications of his behaviour on others, particularly his grandchildren. He and his daughter were very determined to label his son-in-law a violent man simply because he advocated against violence, in general, and particularly, their violent behaviours, and criticised all their glorification of the violent acts they perpetrate.

On the day of the appeal court hearing in August 2015, the wife came up with new dramatic stories as the appeal court requested a retrial because it deemed the conviction by the Magistrate court unsafe. In one of her fanciful stories, perhaps borrowed from Nollywood which she is addicted to, she told the crown court that when her husband was assaulting her, he sat on her and she 'passed out,' but even though she passed out, she could still hear him saying and pleading, "Please don't die; please don't die." She then was said to have told the court, in a funny twist, "I don't want anything bad to happen to him."

When she was asked by her husband's Barrister why such passing out did not show up anywhere else, both in her initial statement to the police and the magistrate court hearing, she replied, "It depends on the line of questioning." The Barrister enquired as to the line of questioning that gave rise to her volunteering such new information of high significance and asked her whether she was someone that made up things as she went along. She got to a stage in court when it became evident to her that initial statement to the police, where she even claimed that her husband had parked out but was allowed to visit at times, her evidence in the Magistrate Court, and her evidence in the Crown Court on the same incident were all different, she broke down in court crying.

The husband was of the view that she cried either because she mistook the court to represent some section of her community who agreed to whatever she says with tears in her eyes or she suddenly realised that all her lies had caught up with her. The court had to go on a brief break to allow her time to gather herself. When the husband took to the witness box and narrated how he was attacked on the day of the incident and previous attacks to which police did nothing, the Crown Court Justices turned down a request to even see some character references from colleagues and friends who had known the husband in the past. The Court found the husband's version of events was believable and decided the case in his favour.

The husband worked as a Locum Mental Health Professional and registered his limited company at the company house. He put his wife's name as a co-director and opened a joint business account in the event of an emergency, not that his wife who has her own employment was doing anything to generate income to his company but in order to protect the interest of his family. The wife, following discussion with her father who advised her to report that she had nothing to do with the company, wrote to company house requesting her name be removed.

On 28th February 2015, she resigned as a director of the company. However, her name remained on the joint account. Whilst her husband was no longer living in the family home and footing up bills elsewhere, he was still paying the house rent and funding high legal bill for solicitors and barristers. His ex-wife was only acting as a witness to the state and maintaining two jobs, but she also went to Child Support Agency to seek more money. When she went to Child Support Agency, her husband had to terminate the rent payment, and on 4th July 2015, she went to the bank and withdrew £10,000 from a business she had resigned from as a director in February. Her actions meant severe financial burden on the company to fulfil its legal obligations. She went about making claims that the company owed her £24,000. She had no clue that even if it was true that she was owed such an amount, she had to pursue it through legal means, not to go and withdraw money from a company she had resigned from.

Following her loss at the Crown Court, both she and her father embarked on a mission to mask their embarrassment and shame having been caught out in their lies and fabrications. Her father, who is a member of People's Club in Nigeria and believes in bribing people for titles and favours (just like buying for the statement he obtained from Nigerian Police in support of her daughter's case), got her to become a member of the same club in London. A male friend of hers, who enrolled her to the Labour Party with a promise to make her a counsellor and pushed her forward to become the secretary to the then mayor of her Local Council, used his connection with the owner of a local newspaper outfit that gives Award to Africans to obtain an award for her.

A few people who had insight into this woman's behaviour wrote to the newspaper demanding to know how she got the award. They demanded to know who nominated her, who her competitors for the award were, and the criteria for such award, especially as it refers to Africa's Best. They also demanded to know the justification for such award to an unworthy character, but the newspaper did not respond. These were all in their quest to mask their shame, cover up their mediocrity, and carry on as though nothing happened.

She then embarked on the anonymous use of social media to campaign against her ex-husband. She started sending anonymous comments to those she perceived as friends to her ex-husband, accusing him of being a 'wife beater' and suggesting that he would have ended up in prison if not that she refused to attend the Crown Court. She got her few friends to carry a hate campaign against her ex-husband, claiming that he is 'a woman hater.'

At a point, she branded him 'a gay,' and began to seek avenues to become friends with men who are friends to her ex-husband. To some, she would present as an abused, helpless and needy woman; to others, she would present herself and her father as unfortunate innocent people and use that as a means of getting information and demanding more money whilst using the children as frontiers. She went about saying that her ex-husband was paying little in child support. She would not tell anyone that she made away with £10,000 from her ex-husband's business account, caused him to spend close to £12,000 in legal fees, stole all the dollars, Euros, expensive wristwatches, and all the valuables when the police deceitfully handed her keys to her ex-husband's room. She did not give a damn about the fact that her ex-husband was having to incur more expenses wherever he was living and needed time to resettle.

Furthermore, she was still maintaining two jobs, and she failed to ask herself where she would get these monies from if her ultimate aim of getting her ex-husband to lose his job was successful. She got one of her friends, who also has violent tendencies and censored by Labour party for threatening to slap someone, to post the following on social network:

"15th of January 2014 is a date when a man came back unannounced from work. Cut the land phone. Went upstairs to batter his wife. Picture evidence available. Police was called who came and found wife in pool of blood. Husband had fled the scene but case was progressed to court by CPS.

"I can post picture evidence as I have been given permission. Found guilty the 1st time at magistrate court but got off on appeal on technicality, does not mean that the offense did not happen. This same mania is parading himself as a credible member of our community plus targeting and preying on women.

"Back off or I will seek an injunction against you from my place of work.

"As a Domestic Violence Lead Member in Waltham Forest for years, I have zero tolerance for men who beat their wife to a point of near death. I will speak out from now on and present photographic evidence which are quite disturbing."

The woman who posted this had alleged previously that this man had written on social network that all the women who are getting awards were getting them by using "**bottom power**." A language this man had made clear he had never spoken, let alone put down in writing before. She also claimed to have the evidence but refused to produce it. Every attempt made by the man (including reporting the matter to the elders of the community) to get her to produce her evidence and right her own wrongs, she refused to answer.

The leader of elders in their community later wrote to the man and said, **"... Regarding our last meeting and discussion. I have finally spoken to Anne, and she's not willing for us to meet over the matter raised. Let's talk in cause of the day ..."** However, she continued to spread malicious rumours about this man and sought to recruit people to join her campaign in support of her friend. Unfortunately for her, some of the women she spoke to about the man and wanted to join the bandwagon happened to know this man and brought this to his attention. When the man raised the issue with this lady in question, she dismissed them as 'mere rumour' and highlighted her bribery instincts by sending the man this text:

"Don't forget the favour I did you with the land deal saving you 5% of total cost in commission as I took nothing from you. This is your attitude of gratitude. Thank you from you for my genuine good heart and generosity. God is the judge and he vindicates. Please do not call me again with hear say and petty gossips. You were billed to receive an award in Waltham Forest next month during our independence celebration alongside others but I am clearly striking you out. Enough is enough."

The man wants to have it on record that on no occasion did he ask this woman to help him with land purchase; rather, she brought up the issue and convinced the man, **"This is very genuine, you only need to pay this amount and give details of your name and postal address and documents will be posted to you. There will be no ifs or buts, and if there is, I will pay back your money, to a penny."** But to the man's surprise, since completing payment in December 2015 and to the time of completing this book in December 2016, the deal's still not been fully completed. Rather, the man is being asked to pay another 60,000 naira before all his documents will be ready. Even though he is willing to pay this amount as the last amount, he is told that the office of 'surveyor general' of Imo State is holding things up. This woman seems to have forgotten that she pledged to refund all the money "to a penny" if there is any "ifs or buts"; instead, she is claiming that she did the man (who would happily take his money back) a favour. This aside, is it not surprising that someone who is a 'Domestic Violence Lead Member in Waltham Forest for years' wants to give an award to someone she believes is a perpetrator of domestic violence? Wonders never cease to happen!

Going back to the case in question, the man's ex-wife, having known how important communication was for him, especially when it comes to their children, began to use the children to maximum effect. She stopped the children from attending the church they had all attended until her father convinced her to revert back to Roman Catholic. She turned their first son, whom she swore will serve as a witness, completely against the husband. She even tried to use him by bringing him to court in the hope that he can witness his father sent to prison on a false premise. She gave all the children maximum freedom and painted the man a bad father. She stopped the little one from seeing his father, claiming that only a court order would make her change her mind. The man, knowing that this was her bid to have him go and spend more money in court and the fact that he was still in the process of settling down, did not feel it was worth his while to go through that at that stage. She would do everything to stop the little boy from seeing his father, even when in public gathering. Twice she has had to snatch the little child from his father's arm, causing the boy severe distress.

Little over one year later, the man was out of the scene, his fear about the influence of his then father-in-law and wife began to come through. The things that never used to occur when the man was living in the house began to happen. One of their children faced expulsion from school for being part of a mob that attacked a school girl. That girl could easily have been beaten to death. This is why an unruly child is not just a risk to self but a risk to security at large.

Their other son was suspended from school for asking another student to verbally abuse a teacher. The man felt helpless in this situation, because it dawned on him that a parent outside is, at best, a friend, and at worst, non-existent. Only children who want to be parented and a live-in parent who understands the importance of parenting would ensure the non live-in parent can still carry out their role as a parent. It also became obvious that the non live-in parent is primarily there for financial purposes, as in most cases, the children would only make contact when in need of money. As a non live-in parent, it is very difficult to make, let alone impose any rules on the children.

When the man sought to find out from his son who took part in assaulting a girl, he told him that it was his choice to do what he did. The man informed his son that no child, let alone a 14-year-old under his watch, would ever have such choice. On a separate issue, when the same 14-year-old asked his father to bring money as a matter of urgency for the renewal of his passport, his father inquired from him why the matter of renewal of passport had become urgent and asked whether he was travelling. His father told him to come back with the reason why it had become so urgent, but little over five minutes, his other twin brother phoned back and told his father to make the money available, stating, "It is not your business to know" if his brother was travelling. His father sought to know whether he heard him correctly, and he repeated that it wasn't his father's business to know. His father asked him where he was getting that type of language from and he replied, "I got it from my brain." His father advised him to hang up.

This man could not believe what his sons were turning into, and made it a point of duty to highlight these things, because tomorrow, these boys would become someone else's husbands. If they are being brought up in this manner, he queries what they would teach their own children. These were children who understood respect, who knew that violence was not an option, and who understood that, in life, there are lines not to be crossed. However, under the influence of their grandfather and their mother, within less than a year and a half, they were showing signs that would raise concern in any reasonable parent.

The man, through his experience, felt that the system is set up to deal with 'certain' men, even when they have done nothing, let alone when someone says they have done something. He could see all the traps, whether real or unreal. Safety became his main focus and priority. He quickly realised that if he adopts any stance that threatened the uncontrolled 'freedom' the children are having from their mother and grandfather, then their mother and grandfather would be able to use the children to further their goals, which was to ruin his life at all cost. A man who used to fly his children at least three times to their private school in Agbani, Enugu; a man who believed so much in his children, but he had adjusted his thinking to know that when presented with a mat and floor, one has to choose the floor first, because if one goes for the mat and loses the floor, there will be no place to lay the mat. The man very quickly realised that he had to be safe first before anything else.

The man, having also seen other men in similar but different situations, has learnt to tread carefully. He had seen and heard about a man who tried to remain the parent he was inside from the outside by seeking to maintain the same level of discipline he instilled in his children but ended up creating a fertile ground for his estranged wife to exploit; in the end, his estranged wife used the children to get him arrested by getting one of the kids to say that he hit them. Though the case was dropped, the man's experience is not one anyone would wish even on their enemy.

Another case was that of a man whose wife alleged that he was sexually abusing his children and was investigated by Social Services and only got lucky that his children denied such abuse took place; he knew that he had to tread carefully. Of course the man witnessed first-hand when his wife instructed their daughter to call the police for trying to use the kitchen door to prevent her from coming into the kitchen to attack him. This was in spite of the children witnessing her throw her slippers at their father as she gave him a chase and their father tried to use the door to prevent her from coming inside. In her frustration of being unable to get into the kitchen, she instructed their daughter to call the police. She, at first, struggled to justify why she called the police but quickly alleged that an old wound mark on her leg was caused by her husband.

The police happily made their arrest, and in the end, she dropped the case. To prove her lies, she gave a different version of event patterning to this event, which happened at night time on 10th April 2012, in her statement for her non-molestation order. In reference to the incident, she wrote:

"The reason the police arrested the respondent on 10th April 2012 was very clear and verifiable and is contrary to his twisted facts here. The truth is that he came to my room in the early hours of the morning to demand sex as he usually does. When I refused, he started to manhandle me as usual, and I had to cry out to my daughter who was already coming to my room to ascertain why I was screaming. My daughter rushed to the room and saw the pain on my face she called the police. The respondent was arrested by the police, bailed and barred from the house or coming near me."

This is a living proof that this was a woman who has been brainwashed by her father and who has become very reckless in pursuit of saying and/or doing anything to please her father, so long as her husband goes down. Her husband had overheard her once discussing with her friend, as they explored means and areas she could use to get her unwanted husband into trouble. The accusation of rape was one of them, and he reported this plan to the police for their information but became very careful. He resolved that he would not engage in sexual activities with the supposed wife; he rather would go elsewhere.

She began to accuse her ex-husband of sleeping with every woman. Her husband told her that if her father had told her not to sleep with a man who disrespects him, it should not be her business who he chooses to sleep with. Her ex-husband knew that their union was going nowhere but was worried about the children. He did not want her to know that he was aware of the rape trap she had set with her friend. He considered leaving the household but was worried that the influence of his father-in-law, combined with that of his ex-wife, could destroy the children, having seen what his father-in-law has done to his own children.

He was worried about the consequences of leaving the children solely with a mother who believed that there was nothing wrong in swearing in front of her children, because, "after all, the children know swear words already"; a mother who asks, "Does this boy look like a bad boy?" in the weird belief that good or bad is visible on people's faces; a mother who was more interested in claiming that a 100 dollar note one of his son's came back from school with belonged to her than finding out how he got it; a mother who had to collect domestic violence leaflets and gathered her children who have never seen their father approach her in anger, let alone touch her, and telling them that their father was doing all that she read from the leaflet to her, in order to brainwash them to sing from the same song sheet with her; a mother who told her children that the benefits of divorce are iPhone 6 and travelling abroad and a mother and grandfather who believe that when good things happen to them, they orchestrate them, but when anything bad happens, then someone or something else did it, to mention but just a few.

This is a mother whose father brainwashed into believing in all manner of fictitious things and will blame the rest of the world for anything that goes wrong but will claim responsibility, even when they contributed nothing to any good thing that happened in their lives. He led her to believe that she was his wife in his previous life and that her ex-husband was behind his brother's killing of a policeman. When she took a part of the money she illegally withdrew from her ex-husband's business account to fly their children to Nigeria without the ex-husband's knowledge, having lied to her children's school that they were travelling to bury her grandmother who died many years ago, her ex-husband had to demand that the children are checked for any marks, as their grandfather would either get them to drink olive oil or get them to go through one kind of ritual or another. He felt stuck between a rock and a hard place.

In their over 18 years' relationship, the husband states that she never celebrated his birthday, though at times she would buy a card and perfume. She had equipped herself with excuses for not doing what she ought to do or someone or something to blame for her own shortcomings. However, he continued to celebrate hers in different ways, and she continued to accept and enjoy them. He would sometimes organise a surprise celebration at another friend's house, present her with her gifts at home and pretend he wanted her to accompany her to their friend's house without knowing that people had gathered there. On one occasion, he rented a limousine to take her, her friends, and the children around London. He believed that if not for the negative influence of her father, they would have made something out of their union, in spite of her very ill-informed upbringing which was neither her fault nor her siblings'.

He only began to have a sexual relationship with her after she pleaded and showed some remorse about what she had been doing. She noted that it was the devil, and that led to them having another child in 2013. But the arrival of her father who was secretly visiting and later was caught hiding in the back garden on 30th April 2014 kick started another episode that led to the final breakup in 2015. She later even accused the ex-husband, in one of her statements for seeking an injunction and molestation order, that he raped her to have the latest child.

In another text she sent to her ex-husband, she accused him of raping someone when he worked for Camden but claimed that at the time, due to the lack of technology, he wasn't prosecuted. She also stated that the ex-husband was dismissed from Seminary school because he raped a girl whilst at the Seminary. She failed to write about a story she once told her husband about her brother who impregnated an under-aged girl in England and had his first daughter through that pregnancy, but her family used their scaremongering and violent tactics to frighten the young girl and suppress the matter.

The ex-husband did not know what to make of her fictitious claims. This is a woman who was said to have spat at her ex-husband in the presence of visitors, threw objects at him, tore up his clothes and poured water on him when he had done little or nothing, let alone attempts to have sex without her consent? She would accuse her husband by saying that he always wants things to go his own way. An example of her husband wanting things his way was when her husband returned from a family reunion held in California, with gifts for his wife from his niece who had never met his wife before.

Having handed the gift to his wife and supplied his niece's number in the hope that she would call, at least to acknowledge receipt, let alone say thanks; she failed to call. After two days, the man asked his wife whether she had called his niece, and like many other times, she said 'no.' The man had to call his father-in-law before she agreed to make the call. However, his wife complained bitterly to her father over the phone: "It is his way or no other way." The man found these allegations frustrating as he believed that showing gratitude when one receives should be standard even for children, let alone adults. The crime this man committed was to advise his wife to acknowledge receipt of the presents for her own image, as someone who shows gratitude when someone else goes out of their way to buy gifts for them. The man wanted his niece to know that her gifts got to the desired destination, not somewhere else.

It is important to note that, all these were sanctioned by this woman's father who currently is playing, if not a huge role, some role in the upbringing of five children (four boys) and (a girl) belonging to this ex-couple. As one cannot teach old dog new tricks, it is only obvious what he would be passing to these children, especially the boys. This is a man who has no understanding of the various implications of his words and actions and various interpretations children may give what he says and does. His daughter also needs to understand and remember that she has four boys. Heaven knows what she would wish on any woman that connives with her father or mother to do the types of things she has connived and done with her father, to any of her sons when they get married. It is likely she would use the same tactics as she and her family deployed in rescuing her brother who impregnated an under-aged girl in England.

This is a woman whose brother abandoned his children, one of which he had with a minor and three he had with a woman he is currently married to in London and went, and secretly married another woman (thereby committing bigamy) and had another child in a different country whilst deceiving and collecting money from his wife in London, who solely is looking after his children. Such a woman has no right to criticise let alone, talk about men whose children can contact...men who are always ready to respond to their children's need if they're not being prevented, brainwashed and used for selfish ends. In addition, if the children have not been presented with some 'wanna-be fathers' to collude with the entire game of using every available means to discredit the man.

Such a woman and her supporters should be ashamed of themselves especially, the woman's entire family who are in total support of what her brother is doing. There are real evil families in this world but it is their supporters who are evil like them, that are the real scums of this earth.

In all these, the man who was the abused remains of the view that men who perpetrate violence against women, whether in a domestic setting or outside, are also the scums of this earth and must be fished out and severely punished. He feels sorry for all genuinely abused women whose suffering and pain are jeered at and made a mockery of by such a woman (thank goodness they are in minority) who, in pursuit of her father's happiness, went all out to fabricate lies, pretending to be a sufferer of domestic abuse when she was, in all honesty, a perpetrator of not only domestic violence but violence outside. She today, has a police warning against her for threatening another woman who she believed was having an affair with her ex-husband.

The man is calling on society to continue to deal with men who are destroying children through their violent activities on their mothers but at this same time pleads that, the needs of some men who are at the receiving end of such violence are not ignored for any reason whatsoever. Injustice is always maintained if the goal is to hold the oppressor/s on the rebound. He also asks that the police should not be under pressure to deliver plausible statistics or become over interested in promotion, because any miscarriage of justice against one is a miscarriage of justice against all.

The man also queries how people can be held liable if they offer an un-prescribed medication to a vulnerable person but society turns a blind eye when someone withdraws from a vulnerable person, a prescribed medication for their own health and safety and the health and safety of others especially, when such act results in not only the murder of an individual but also attempted murder of others? The man also queries how withdrawing a prescribed medication from a vulnerable adult and replacing it with olive oil does not amount to giving that vulnerable adult an un-prescribed substance and withdrawal of appropriate treatment? Shouldn't it be standard that the individual responsible for such an act should be given the opportunity to explain their act, if not for anything else, it would act as a warning to other people who may be so inclined or in the business of doing such things?

In all, what this man, went through and continues to go through highlights some hidden facts relating to domestic abuse which takes many forms and shapes. Therefore, in order to get things right, each case needs to be properly studied and understood and the law should, and must, cut both ways. The questions to consider are: What would have happened to this man if he did not have the funds to appeal this case? How many people have been condemned in this fashion because they could not afford to pursue a redress? What does the future hold for humanity if this type of injustice continues to be swept under the carpet? Is humanity going to keep covering up these social ills for the children to repeat, thinking it is the right way to go? Must it happen to everyone before we wake up to the prevailing injustice in our society?

It is critical to note that this man was suspended from work when his ex-wife made the first allegation in 2012, and it took months before his employers reinstated him. This caused the man to lose substantial income and caused him a lot of emotional distress. The second time around, the employers, having seen this man come into work in wet clothes and other times torn clothes and seen pictures of bites, his room turned upside down and seen a picture of his ex-wife standing on the gate with her back facing the camera—as she did not want her face to be seen—when she was blocking the entry gate, plus the fact that his ex-wife had threatened one of his colleagues, decided to back the man.

In spite of police effort to ruin this man's career by quickly sending a DBS that read, "Charged for battery," and the magistrates court's verdict, his employers, who have recorded no untoward incident against this man in his many years of service and have witnessed this man come to work with bite wounds, torn and wet clothes, decided to risk assess the man's work and made a firm decision to wait for the outcome of the appeal ruling. Even after this man was cleared on appeal court, the same police who were quick to condemn the man took almost one year to clear his DBS.

Something is definitely wrong with any system where it is clear that one is set out to maliciously destroy another, yet they are ignored or subtly encouraged to keep trying to invent something until the innocent is either nailed wrongly or becomes psychologically tortured and destroyed. What many don't realise is that, whether an allegation is founded or not, vindication is not an event but a painful and costly process that has severe material and psychological consequences to the wrongly accused. The malicious accuser goes scot-free in readiness to do more without even a warning. To date, this woman is still threatening violence.

As stated earlier, she had violently snatched their youngest child from the hands of her ex-husband in public, and in the last episode, she threatened that she would slap her ex-husband and will become violent if he ever carries the little child without going to court to make arrangements. The ex-husband remains of the view that he can only do that when he is settled and have enough money to pursue another court case.

In the meanwhile, she's left to play it as she chooses without any consideration on the child's psychological well-being. She remains only interested in her self-gratification, without inkling to the child's emotional welfare. The violent snatching of the little boy that caused him much distress and threat of violence was again reported to the police, and to date, apart from the ex-husband being contacted by the police for further details, no one has come back to say whether she has been spoken to. The ex-husband is fully aware that the only trap she has to set now is all to do with using the children.

Justice can only be equitable when it is not only the accused but the accuser and the entire systems involved in the prosecution of the accused are on trial.

The truth is, when one is cohabiting with someone who wants them to do the wrong thing, the person is in trouble either way. It is either the person gets into trouble by doing that which is wrong or be in trouble with the person they live with for insisting on doing the right thing. This man perhaps would have lived in 'peace' with his wife if he agreed that his brother-in-law killed someone because someone else did black magic on him, not because he was asked to stop his medication and replace it with olive oil by his father. If he agreed to that, the family could pursue a claim against the Local Authority responsible for his care and treatment for negligence. If he joined in the celebration of violent acts prompted by his then father-in-law, of course there would be a temporary 'peace' if he ignored and remained silent to everything and played along with everything as laid down by his then father-in-law. Humanity needs a closer look if the wrongs of our world can be corrected.

Humanity needs to appreciate the fact that life is meant to be orderly. Any life that is not orderly is a disordered life. If the life of a parent is disordered, their children are likely to follow suit, because children can only replicate, reduce, or enhance behaviours seen or heard. Parenting is all about partnership, collaboration, complement, and teamwork. No one should go into such if they want to play on their own, and no one should partner anyone who believes in 'your side, my side, let's see who the children will follow.' Parenting is not a competition, challenge, or popularity contest. In parenting, both those who create opportunities to be controlled and those who seek to control them are guilty. If a partnership is not based on mutual respect, understanding and effective communication then go happily single all the way.

Remember, when children cannot account for the whereabouts of their resident parent/s, they follow suit and often with devastating consequences. Political correctness cannot help but hinder humanity. We must learn to embrace the truth and call a spade a spade; else children may wish to eat it thinking it is bread.

Read below information supplied to me by Mrs. Adenuga. This is a letter from a death row inmate to his mother. Though the letter refers to his mother, there are fathers who encourage and support bad behaviours in their children as we can note above from a father who says, "Some people are born to take risks." In the end, when things go wrong, the same parents would seek to blame the rest of the world for their self-inflicted woes.

A death row inmate awaiting execution asked, as a last wish, a pencil and paper. After writing for several minutes, the convict called the prison guards and asked that this letter be handed to his biological mother. The letter said "...Mother, if there were more justice in this world, we would be both executed and not just me. You are as guilty as I am for the life I led. Remind yourself when I stole and brought home the bicycle of a boy like me? You helped me to hide the bicycle so my father did not see it. Do you remember the time I stole money

from the neighbor's wallet? You went with me to the mall to spend it. Do you remember when I argued with my father and he's gone? He just wanted to correct me because I stole the final result of the competition and for that I had been expelled. Mom, I was just a child, shortly after I became a troubled teenager and now I'm a pretty malformed man. Mom, I was just a child in need of correction, and not an approval. But I forgive you!

I just want this letter to reach the greatest number of parents in the world, so they can know what makes all people, good or bad...is education. Thank you mother for giving me life and also helping me to lose it."

Advice to married, unmarried, and divorced people who are looking

It is important to make a decision today and have a zero tolerance for verbal and/or physical threat of violence, whether inside or outside your home, to your person or someone else. Do not condone, tolerate, or accept it for any reason whatsoever.

The second is stealing. You need to do whatever it takes legally to stop those who use any means or excuse to own what is not theirs. A thief is often a selfish person who can be stealing from you, even though you live together as a couple. Stealing takes numerous forms; from stealing physical cash to not contributing financially to projects of the household.

Be careful not to be in union with such individuals, unless you are like-minded people, but then, you are likely to be sleeping with 'one eye open' and your children are likely to copy to a devastating effect. Upon violence and stealing hang all the evils of our time, and those who condone these for whatever reason, alongside the perpetrators, are the scums of this earth.

No marriage is meant to be easy, and no two marriages are the same. Ensure that you do not marry because others are getting married or because of the following: you are under pressure from your parents to get them grandchildren, you are after good looks only, you are after someone's deep pocket, you're still over intoxicated with single lifestyle or not ready to leave your parents and become an independent adult.

Marry only when you are ready and marry someone you are compatible with. **Be sure you're certain of your would-be partner's belief systems; this is very critical.**

Marry someone that adds value to your life and someone you share a lot in common with.

No matter your infatuation, never jump into marriage with your eyes closed.

Make sure you ask many, many questions and receive many answers.

Do the best to know what you are letting yourself into before agreeing to marry.

Bear in mind that the crisis in our world originates from families and the genesis of every family is the couple at the root of it.

It helps a great deal to know the background of the individual you wish to share your life with, because an apple doesn't fall far from an apple tree. People often grow to replicate what they observed. Never compare your marriage to anyone else's, because yours is different. And never depart from your marriage, especially where there are children, unless your health and/or safety is being compromised. Marriage, like every good thing, does not come easy; therefore, requires work and dedication to get it right. In the end, it is not necessarily love that keeps marriages but compromise and understanding. The consequences of getting the wrong partner, especially when children are involved, can be grave. As a result, look very well before you leap.

Finding the 'right' person first time around may not be so difficult but be warned: it is very difficult second time around, unless the third party existed prior to the dissolution of the first one. Even at that, there is every likelihood that what one observed whilst keeping two relationships will become different when the nature of the relationship changes. The act of keeping two relationships going at the same time is not advisable, because anyone who operates in such a fashion is likely to have a third party operating in the second marriage too, and anything is possible. It is also advisable that no one in a marriage should step outside of that marriage or encourage the other through emotional or physical abuse to seek comfort and/or love elsewhere. At times, extramarital affairs are by-products of emotional deprivation locked into complex domestic business ties. It is all so easy to say 'cut clean' and start a new relationship. The reality is often different when children and other commitments are involved.

In spite of all said, finding a partner second time around is much more difficult, because when one encounters what they perceive as a snake, anything that is long or crawls like a snake becomes a suspect. It is also difficult because of the baggage one carries from the first union, age, and some degree of 'desperation' that makes settling the second time around difficult. Though it is advisable not to compare, as human beings, it is not easy not to compare the first with the second. However, holding the new one who has nothing to do with the past on a rebound must not be the case. But there are serious things that should not be ignored.

From second marriages upwards, it's likely that either parties or one party have children. If, for any reason, you do not fancy your new partner having or maintaining a relationship with their children, then you may need to query why you should be in that relationship. If you are marrying a foreigner and you are constantly worried about language barrier and do not believe that the love they have for you is enough to protect you, then you need to query the need to be in that relationship. If, for any reason, you cannot spare a thought for the other person or accept the other person the way they are then, think carefully before venturing into a second relationship.

Though one is advised to start driving immediately after a motor accident, it is not always advisable to jump into another marriage soon after the first one, unless one is certain where they are going. Coming out of a union when there is no obvious third party propelling it is like suffering a broken leg playing a football match. One needs time to recover and heal up before going back on the pitch.

It cannot be overemphasised that couples need to do whatever it takes to stay in the first unions, especially if children are involved—see "Cohabiting" (Ihenacho 2014). The greener pastures out there are few and far in-between. Therefore, only depart from the first one if there are irreconcilable differences and if verbal and/or physical violence become a part of the equation. Violence of any kind is not, and should not be, a part of any relationship, let alone a loving relationship.

Never depart because those who may have made mistakes and became single pretend to you that they are having a time of their lives due to possible envy and/or in their quest to have 'club members' in the spirit of 'strength in numbers.' Know it that even many drivers of separation are often disappointed, as what they thought or imagined is not always the case.

If you happen to become single again, simply make the best and most of it and do not live a life of regret, but please do not pretend that having a loving relationship in a family environment is not the best, if not for everyone, for most people. Do ensure you do not seek to derail others who are in relationships, especially where children are involved. Be honest to those in relationships and be an advocate for parents living and bringing up their children together in love. Help people to see the pitfalls and encourage marriage, because it is the bedrock of humanity.

Let your experience help not hinder others, and do not be selfish and/or crafty.

It is important to note that everything starts with you and me, it is an illusion that one can be complete on their own. It is an impossibility that one can be happy or create happiness on their own without others. In numerical terms, each of us represents zero, which is all important, as zero represents infinity; however, zero is totally useless on its own. In metaphoric term, each individual, community, or nation represents a hand, and as big and as useful as a hand is, it cannot wash and keep itself clean. Though they sound plausible and at times inspiring, those who say it is all about you are mistaken, as it is neither all about you nor me but all about you and me. Neither the foundation (Me) nor the structure (You) is useful on their own, but both become useful when integrated and complement one another. Until humanity understands this and come away from 'me, myself and I' ideology, our future as tenants to this world will remain in doubt and full of pain and suffering, no matter how we pretend and/or cover up.

It is incalculable the damage that stems from destroying a home, especially as it relates to psychological effects on children who many consider as resilient. What many consider as resilience in children is 'survival instinct,' which masks what is really going on. Children have to be 'resilient' in order to survive and cope with the situation they found themselves. They would not want to upset the live-in parent who they depend on and are likely to suppress their real feelings. The feelings suppressed often come back in later years and manifest itself in different shapes, forms, and ways, depending on the personality of the affected. In many cases, it creates in children serious psychological problems which result in mental health crisis in adulthood.

Watch out for those who, as Christians, would promise heaven and earth to others but would withhold even what others give them to offer to God. Those who would say they are testing someone to see if they can look after them unassisted but already are desperate to confirm the date of marriage. Those who claim to be comfortable but are running from people due to the debt they owe. Those who are living in the hope of things to come, and how things would be better once living together becomes a reality. Be warned that anyone who cannot do anything at the beginning is unlikely to do much in the middle and at the end. Anyone who cannot part with their penny now is unlikely to part with their pounds later.

Organise your life with you in mind primarily, and find someone whose organisation of their own life blends or can blend into yours. Don't organise your life based on someone else or in order to meet expectations of other people, irrespective of who they are. Be stubbornly real to yourself, go at your own pace, and do things at your own time, because if you don't, you will end up living another person's life. Whatever someone else wants you to do, find out first from them why they cannot do that themselves.

Beware, those referred to as 'mums and dads' are often fixated with their biological children, but mothers and fathers are likely to parent any child given the opportunity. If they are willing to take a pound from you for their biological children but cannot part with a penny for yours, then you need to watch it. If they are happy to say, “My children are fine,” but are not able to ask, “How are your children?” insert a question mark. The last thing you want to do is to fail an exam twice. If all they are interested in is themselves and no one else, be careful. If all they can present is their own needs in the deluded belief that you are without needs, watch it too. Fixate yourself with ‘Added Value,’ so long as you are intent on adding value to the other. When one is thirty and over, they need to ensure they are not looking for someone without baggage, because when and if they find one, that person will certainly be the baggage and all the reasons why others have been and run away will soon unravel.

In summary, in every relationship, one needs to ‘seek added value at all times in the areas of care and support. Added values are often not obtainable from the things everyone can naturally do but in the things human beings are nurtured to do. If all one is prepared to give is what anyone can give, where is the added value? A relationship should either keep you the way you are or enhance you; otherwise, there should be no deal. Everyone needs to play their unique part, irrespective of how small, because no matter how big and/or strong a hand is, it can never keep both hands clean on its own.’ It obviously cannot keep itself clean.

At every stage of a relationship, there should always be complementary process at play. Put your very best in any relationship you call your own, no matter how little or big. If one cannot do the little, they are unlikely to do the big. An Igbo adage says, “Ana esi na ushi ahuru mata uto nsi”—meaning “one can sense the taste of faeces from the smell of fart.” Do not be deceived by castles built in the air, for they do not exist. Future plans are good, but no one has ever lived in the future but in the ‘here and now.’

At the stage of divorce, it is expected that people are likely to be carrying some form of baggage. Therefore, discuss the various baggage honestly and ensure the idea is not for one to offload on the other. Rather, to find ways to share in each other’s baggage. The general rule is to take cognisance of the fact that it is not easy to teach an old dog new tricks. Therefore, never indulge in trying to change the other person. Rather, love them as they are and compromise on anything that is not the way you prefer it. In most cases where there needs to be a change, it probably is you that need to change in order for you to see the desired outcome. Seek each other's happiness; seek compatibility, friendship, companionship, and have a time of your lives enjoying yourselves.

Before undertaking any peace mission in families, communities, groups, or nations, do understand that the greatest threat to peace is the 'off the shelf' peace, fake 'quick fix kiss and makeup' peace with quick hand-shake captured in glorious still pictures. This creates the opportunity for the victim to remain vulnerable and gives the perpetrator more teeth to bite, and other angles to explore with devastating consequences.

No tree with rotten root can produce a healthy fruit. Let our actions be inspired and driven by the possible dire consequences of inaction.

Peace is a process, and not an event.

'BLACK' PEOPLE & OVER-REPRESENTATION IN MENTAL HEALTH IN LONDON

According to statistics, "African Caribbean people are more likely to enter the mental health services via the courts or the police, rather than from primary care, which is the main route to treatment for most people. They are more likely to be treated under a section of the Mental Health Act, are more likely to receive medication, rather than be offered talking treatments such as psychotherapy, and are overrepresented in high and medium secure units and prisons." They are also more likely to receive diagnosis such as schizophrenia compared to other ethnic groups.

In England, poor socioeconomic background, immigration, modern technological gadgets, lack of appreciation of cultural differences, and racism contribute adversely and have been blamed for the over-representation of 'black' people in the mental health sector in London, for example. But are these factors not applicable to Asians, Jewish, Chinese, and other communities that migrated to England? If they are, then what is at the root of this for 'black' community?

In the Animal Kingdom, animals calling on one another to scratch their backs are not common place. Other species find alternatives like the trees in order to have their backs scratched. It is primarily a human thing to seek out one another for such scratching, making human beings the 'profound' social animals, interdependent and a brand of species that is totally unique when it comes to interpersonal relationships and dependency. As a result, the mental state of individuals owes a lot to what others are doing, as well as social factors and people's lifestyles. The harmony in families and communities stimulates human beings positively and ensures better and stable mental state in individuals within such families and communities. And the reverse is the case for individuals within disorganised, dysfunctional and broken families and communities. Residual psychological damage gathered from dysfunctional and broken families impact adversely on the relevant communities. The affected children within such environments suffer badly, and this manifests more in adulthood.

Having worked in the mental health sector for over a decade and a half and made at least over one thousand applications for the detention of mental health patients, I can confidently say that over three-quarters of these detentions relate to individuals who route from dysfunctional and/or broken families. In this, three-quarter are people with background histories that state: "... father and mother separated, divorced or one of the parents died when they were young," or "they were brought up in a family riddled with abuse of all kinds."

Being that everyone is susceptible to mental disorder (just like cancer), as everyone carries the gene, the issue then becomes: What makes one more or less susceptible to the disorder? Issues relating to people's lifestyle, losses of all kinds, lack of productivity, limited or non-existent social support systems, and coping mechanisms become pivotal. It is obvious that where families are united, communities function better in a cohesive manner and individuals within such environments strive with better 'feel good factors,' which assures good mental health. Communities such as Asian, Chinese, and Jewish fare better in this regard because they have a culture they believe and adhere to. It is the culture that brings the best or worst out of people. It can unite or disunite communities.

Looking closely at the Jewish community in London, for example; one can see the bond in their family set up and the unity in their community. This is engineered by their culture, which they practice wherever they go. The Jewish culture, from their perspective, plays second fiddle to none, and no Jewish person is above their culture and traditions, irrespective of location and status. Through this bond, they are not only able to succeed as individuals but as a community. In the course of my work, there was a period I worked in an area of London with a large population of Jewish people. Throughout my time working there, I only detained one Jewish man.

In my opinion, there was no other explanation other than the fact that the Jewish community has a culture that serves them well. A Culture that keeps their families and community supported and united. A culture that speaks of togetherness where people complement, collaborate and work in partnership. This ensures that when one has a problem, the problem is shared by many, and "a problem shared is a problem solved." This is similar to the other communities such as Asian and Chinese, where one only needs to put a pound in the pocket of any of these and the pound would circulate amongst the same community at least five times before it comes out into universal circulation.

These communities are not immune to personal and personality clashes and issues amongst individuals and/or groups, but they have mastered the act of pursuing a 'common interest' agenda. Through this 'common interest' agenda, they have been able to set up their own businesses and local economy serving their own people. New migrants from these communities fare better on arrival as they receive genuine support and assistance from their well-structured, designed and tested systems. In these communities, honesty and trust are key. The sellers are not going to rip off the buying members of their community, and the buyers will not be looking to close down the business of the sellers by offering to pay nothing or less than the going price for goods purchased.

Those who want to set up businesses are not only encouraged but supported morally and financially to do so, and they work earnestly to repay any loan borrowed in the knowledge that others depend on their repayments to start theirs. Just like the five fingers, each of these communities is independent, strong and healthy. If all communities do the same and bring their unique attributes together in one accord, London will become a beacon to the whole world.

It is unfortunate that the contrast is the case in 'Black' community, where success is primarily an individual rather than a collective community thing. Some highly efficient 'black' professionals treat their fellow 'black' people with contempt, whilst relying on sentiments and emotion as a reason for shabby practise. Stories of 'black' lawyers who would collect money from fellow 'black' people, even though they know that they have no grounds to regularise their stay in England, are out there for all to see. Is it 'black' pastors who continue to ask fellow 'black' people clearly suffering from a mental disorder to 'sow a seed' for their healing, when they know that what they need is antipsychotic medication in order to stabilise their mental state? Is it the fake pastors, seers, and prophets that continue to only see what 'evil' a family member is doing and never see any good a family member does to their family? All these are done in the name of extracting money by deception and manipulation through a weird belief system.

'Black' people collectively represent, if not the malfunctioning 'finger, one of the malfunctioning fingers that is not only depriving itself but forcing others to overcompensate and resulting in the weakening of the overall performance and efficiency of the hand (the world).' They have not managed to separate their individual, interpersonal problems with their collective communal interests. Issues of culture that binds families and communities together are not there; rather, the ones that destabilise families and divide communities are very active in 'black' communities.

Many have argued that, there is a structural agenda that contributes to this malfunction in 'black' community. In many 'black' families, couples who are meant to be working in a complementary, collaborative and collective manner are in the main in competition, contest and challenge with one another. In many 'black' families, good and bad couples live under the same roof because 'popularity contest' is the order of life. Couples who live in the same household who ought to sing from one song book are divided to the extent that when one says no, the other would say yes to the children to prove they are the good or better parent. This same mode of operation then filters and feeds into their community where envy, jealousy, competition, contest, and backbiting are rife.

It is ironic that 'black people' are the main ones visibly carrying the Bible and speak of the love of God but seem to be passionate in the hatred of themselves. Hence they struggle to network and build together. An average fellow 'black' worshipper would rather spend their money in another shop belonging to other ethnicities just to make sure they do not contribute to what they perceive as the success of their fellow 'black' worshipper. Though they are great in public expression of love, hugs, and kiss, inwardly, the story is different. In 'black' community, there is no collective response to problem-solving, no local economy serving the community, no sense of genuine identity, culture, and tradition that is positive for growth.

Each individual is almost an island unto themselves, on their own and the best one would have is a united family, but then, once any social upheaval engulfs such family, there is no adequate community support. The systems in operation in 'black' families and communities breed and nurture mental disorder. It is these that contribute most to the over-representation of 'black' people in not only mental health but graveyards and prisons.

Many who think that patriotism means 'masking or minimising the obvious' need to know that a good parent is never ashamed to do whatever it takes to expose their ill child to treatment, whilst a bad parent seeks to mask the illness in pretence that "all is well" or "my child is not the only one ill; leave my child alone" to a devastating conclusion.

Many children brought up in 'black' families are as confused as anything, as they witness their parents sing from different song sheets. Many are brought up in families rife with all manner of abuse, where parents are using every available legal means to get at the other. Today, due to the ills in black families, many young professional 'black' women in England are struggling to find young 'black' male equivalent to marry.

Some parents want to use the law enforcement agencies to proof to their children who the 'power' belongs to, without knowing that they are destroying themselves and their children in the process. The children in these households have no refuge inside and have no community to turn to for help. They then rely on peers in the same situation as them for support which is like the 'blind leading the blind' to devastating effect. In many 'black' families, parents act like 'two separate hands' that know little or nothing of what each other is doing.

At times children have no clue about the whereabouts of their parents. When a child cannot find love and relative peace at home, they seek it outside and, at times, with devastating consequences. The psychological trauma many children in 'black' families go through are impossible to calculate or articulate. This trauma can result in many crises and dependency on illicit substances and the relative 'safety' and 'comfort' joining of gangs could momentarily give them. These are recipes for disaster and open wide not only the gates of mental illness but the graveyards and prisons to 'black' people.

In a particular 'black' ethnic group, every structure meant to unite families and communities instigate destabilisation in families. Even in their religious settings—as some of their prophets and pastors only see family members responsible for the woes of other family members, but to date, have never seen family members responsible for anything good that happened to any family member. Some of these religious leaders preach that their members can only be 'the head,' not 'the tail,' and 'only good,' and nothing bad will happen to their members, as everything bad is not their 'portion.'

Many, according to Mrs. Ify Adenuga, Skepta, Jason, JME, and Julie Adenuga's mother, take Chieftaincy titles and are called "Ogbu Agus"—meaning "killers of Lions"—when many, if not all, of them have never seen a Lion live. The level of malfunction in that ethnic group which stems from the dysfunction and breakdown in families is frightening to behold. A typical state of illusion, anomie, and confusion where people struggle to relate to the fact that good can never exist without bad, there's no head without a tail, and everybody has to be different for the world to go round.

Here lies the problem: black people and over subscription in mental health. When your foundation is broken, you are likely to be broken too. People respond to the particular culture that defines them. Any culture that does not support and respect family unity and community cohesion would generate malfunction, which results in high levels of mental disorder. The psychological impact of family breakups and dysfunctional families on children is incalculable, and they often manifest in later years. Without strong families, there will be no community cohesion and, as social animals, human beings are not meant to survive and/

or prosper on an individual basis without collaboration with others. The individuals within a broken and malfunctioning community will be more susceptible to mental disorder, period!

Some Africans and Caribbean people have been conditioned to be not only lazy, but also too dependent. Hence they are likely to blame Satan or other people for their own self-orchestrated woes and depend on pastors and other fellow human beings to take them to the same God they call their Father. They negate the WILL given to each and every one of them to be architects of their own destinies. They forget that they are each on this planet with their respective and unique voices and assignments to perform.

Every day they expect miracles to happen and others to come and solve their own problems. Yes, as individuals, many of them have achieved so much and are upright in their reasoning but structurally, culturally, and collectively, they have performed poorly and have almost become a laughing stock. **Their collective malfunction and backwardness have not only cost them dearly, but they have also deprived humanity enormously.** They have no clue that their real strength, survival, and contribution to humanity lies with what they do as a collective body.

The majority of their governments and individuals who are 'doing well' are so selfish they have ignored the rest without building a platform for each individual child to be the best they can be. They have no clue that the reason why people from other continents are respected and not taken for granted is because of their economic and political strength both at home and abroad. They have become masters of the 'MARCH,' as all they do is to march following any incidents of murder of a 'black' person. Instead of working together, supporting, patronising and encouraging one another and, through that, build their own economy serving their own people like other communities, they are busy infighting and carrying the Bible, preaching love but do not show it in action towards themselves.

All they seem to be good at is spreading evil, malicious and unfounded rumours about others whilst masquerading, recruiting 'birds of a feather,' and playing to the galleries for selfish and wicked purposes. Another thing they are good at is jostling for positions, seeking to be the head without the tail, and without knowing that it is difficult for the head to survive without the tail, and without querying what will become of a body that is all heads or what will happen to all heads without the body. These 'delusional' attributes bring a generational curse, as African children copy in order to replicate.

In the end, they crown and mask everything with a verse or two from the scripture. This is sickening indeed, and the quicker they tell themselves the truth, the better for them and humanity. They may, however, decide to continue wallowing in ignorance. The choice is theirs. Their malfunction as an entity which deprives them of collective and communal support is the real reason they are disrespected, overrepresented in mental health services, prisons, and graveyards.

SUCCESS AND FAILURE

It is a known fact that the easiest thing in life is to blame others for one's shortcomings. Blame is usually associated with failure. This is a mechanism human beings use to absolve themselves of any responsibility, to ensure they are not standing alone in their shame, and to seek vindication. Blame very rarely occurs when success is achieved, as human beings are very quick to point to their achievement in a successful venture. The reverse should be the case because, as stated earlier, success demands one's one hundred percent commitment and effort as a minimum, but relies heavily on other people in order for it to happen. In order to achieve that one hundred percent, one must sacrifice a lot, for there is no success without sacrifice.

It is important for everyone to examine what they consider as their success. Is it in academics? Could they have achieved it without being taught or without being in good health? Is it in business? One could own all the shops in the entire world, but one would never count them as successful if customers do not patronise them. Are you the owner or chief executive officer of a company? Are you the brain with all the ideas behind the success of a company? The truth is, your ideas can never work or be useful if people do not buy into or implement them, just as 'the brain' said to the rest of the body parts, "I could have given the best advice, but if the rest of you rejected it or refused to implement it, the advice would have meant nothing." Is your success in politics?

No one can hold any elected office without others helping them and people voting them in. In fact, some of the best politicians cannot make it into government because they do not have the right people around them and could not package and market their brand properly. Examine the history of one of life's celebrated individuals, Nelson Mandela. As the world honours, celebrates, mourns and recounts all his achievements through personal sacrifice in service to humanity, Mr. Mandela in his wisdom and humility was the first to share his achievements with all those who made it possible, including ex-president F.W. de Klerk. He recognised that without this kind of person/s, none of what he set out to achieve would have been possible. He was also not oblivious to his failings as a human being. Hence he said, "I am a sinner who kept on trying," as he reminded those wishing to make him a saint.

Is your success being a football star? Many of the better footballers have not even been noticed by the right people, let alone signed up by a club. Is your success to do with an appointment? One very rarely appoints oneself, but usually, one would rely on someone to appoint them. What is your success? Examine it properly and discover that it is not something an individual can achieve alone. However, success demands one's 100% effort and commitment as a minimum. This effort and commitment (on its own) will never be enough to achieve success, but it will form the basis upon which success is achieved when others subscribe to it. Hence humility is required in order to be really successful, as it is not all about the individual's effort.

Failure is one of those things in life that one happily achieves on one's own, either by doing what comes naturally or doing nothing at all. Failure is resident within everyone, that's why one does not need to do anything or go anywhere to keep it; but success lives far away, and one must work hard and obtain other people's help in order to reach where success lives, let alone obtain it. Therefore, success is what should be shared, as it is not solely individually attained like failure—which is individually owned. Success is a team effort, and failure an individual's lack of effort or effort others did not subscribe to. However, immature and undeveloped emotion led Adam and many people today to turn this glaring reality upside down: people are quick to attribute their well-earned failure to others, and collective success to themselves. In other words, there is no such thing as a self-made person.

MIXED REACTION FOLLOWING RECEIPT OF AWARD

I was greatly honoured and humbled to have received a recognition award for Community Leadership from 'Women Aspiring Great Success' (WAGS) during their Charity Ball & Recognition Award Ceremony 2016 held in Luton on 16th July 2016. I was more humbled and had to pinch myself in humility when someone said to me:

"Did you realise that you are the only Nigerian amongst Zimbabweans and a handful of African nationals (amongst whom was our awesome and inspirational Dr. Pauline Long, a Kenyan but honorary Nigerian) to have been honoured tonight? I found your speech very, very inspirational..."

However, I do insist that, though I was born an Igbo man from the Eastern Region of Nigeria and have lived in Britain more than I lived in Igbo land, I belong to the one human race, one human family, and I am a full-fledged tenant of this world we are all renting and must all depart, whether we like it or not. I want to stress that I am neither superior nor inferior to anyone, and can only serve as a part of the jigsaw puzzle which becomes redundant and useless on its own, just like you.

Amidst my excitement, I felt ashamed of our world and its confused leadership when the founder of this noble charity (Everjoy Kurangwah) addressed the audience, highlighting the plight of many African women whose dignity have been badly exposed, ignored and neglected to the extent that they are using leaves for sanitary towels. In a world that is well resourced, where many dress up and parade themselves as statesmen and women. It is an embarrassing situation so shameful that I would not have legs to stand on proclaiming myself as a leader, irrespective of the nation I represent. Yet, many ask why our world is in a meltdown.

In recognition of this awful state of affair in a world of plenty, I dedicated my award to all the girls and women who have been damaged by awful parenting and society at large. Isn't it a dreadful shame that men who laid the foundations of our world were clever enough to realise that 'children are the future' but foolish to damage and relegate the needs of those who not only incubate but lay the foundations for these children (women) under normal circumstances? Even an irrational mind understands the importance of foundations to houses and plants, let alone children who are the future leaders of our world.

I have seen the generational impact of both sound and damaged mothers respectively ... intelligent and morally sound mothers versus violent and troublesome mothers who primarily are by-products of the terrible foundations laid by men. Our world, indeed humanity, can only get to the promised land when human beings become rational and make the needs of the girl child (the source of life) paramount.

In support of this noble and humane cause, I make this pledge: 5% of the proceeds of this book, as stipulated earlier, goes to WAGS to help in reaching out to the affected women.

Positive Approach

In all walks of life, as in all corners of the world, good and bad eggs exist. However, just like a goalkeeper's mistake can be more costly to a team compared to that of a midfielder, the bad eggs in certain areas of work have a more devastating impact on humanity more than the good ones. It is often the few bad eggs that dictate the suffering of the rest. Many restrictions and difficulties humanity has suffered are as a result of what the few are doing wrong. There are certain areas in life where these few bad eggs acting like poor 'goalkeeper' generate untold damage to humanity. These areas are: criminal justice system, law enforcement agencies, healthcare, education, politics, religion, and mass media.

In my personal life, I have seen and experienced the good and bad within these areas of human endeavours. It is important to highlight the attitude expected of anyone wishing to operate within the above-mentioned fields of human endeavour. In the course of my work as an Approved Mental Health Professional, I have come across many wonderful and well-meaning police officers, but one, in particular, impressed me the most when he told me, "I read a lot of awful things about the police force in the media and decided to join to help make a positive difference." This is the approach and attitude anyone aspiring to serve the public needs to have in order to reverse the awful trend humanity is currently in.

Having said all this, the vital thing for everyone to bear in mind is that everyone arrives into this world empty. No one is bad or good at birth. Even though everyone has individual threats in terms of their respective personalities, everything a child does or says stems from something seen or heard, because even imagination and inspiration stem from something already in existence. This makes parenting and early experiences of a child the most critical period of everyone's journey on earth. The foundation laid during one's formative years is critical to what one ends up becoming in life. Many have cited peer pressure and the screens children watch as major contributing factors, but those peers and makers of those screens were all by-products of parenting too. In view of this, the person one cohabits with becomes paramount as they contribute immensely to what would happen to the formation of offspring from that union.

To all individuals, families, religious groups, communities, and nations that make up this one entity called the world, I say, irrespective of the position one occupies within this broad spectrum, let each of us remember that we are all called to serve, learn and share from one another. We all need to see where each of us is going wrong and not only see where others are going wrong. We then need to focus more on making right our own wrongs in the knowledge that errors not identified will never be corrected but only repeated. If we fixate ourselves on blaming others for our own woes, our woes will continue unabated.

For those whose talent are celebrated and those who see themselves as heads, I say, never forget that being at the top does not make you exclusive, as no fruit stays on top of the tree without a base and no head hangs without the body supporting it. You need to remember that without others, you can never be where you are, as you cannot stand on your own. In view of this, humility and mutual respect, not exclusivity and arrogance, are all you need. Even in medical profession where hierarchy and superiority reigns supreme, it is important that those practising medicine appreciate that a medical student has something in them to offer the most 'senior' medical practitioner given the respect, not fear, each person deserves.

Remember, no matter how big a finger is, it can never do the job of the smallest one and can never do the job required of the hand on its own. It will also require assistance, at a point or another, from the small one as the small one would require from it. Let each of us wake up to our roles and responsibility in the knowledge of the fact that any feeling of superiority or inferiority towards any individual, community, religious group, or nation is indicative of psychological deformity, because such concepts are not applicable where there are differences meant for one another's benefit.

As big as the "radiator is, it cannot say the small plug is inferior, neither will the small plug say the radiator is superior," for both are different for specific reasons and are called to serve with mutual respect. All the evils of our world stem from the deformed psychological application of superiority and inferiority to unequal but equally important human beings. **Our world needs to adopt a stance which stipulates that in a world of inevitable and vitally important differences, any individual or group that wishes death on another because they are different is deluded and has lost the right to live. In all said and done, bearing in mind what the small plug represents in a huge engine and the unequal but equally important fingers, all we need is respect, not fear, which should be reciprocal, irrespective of which end of the spectrum one occupies. As a result, any thought, feeling, or agenda by any individual, religious group, community, or nation that spells or speaks of superiority or inferiority is ill-thought out and driven by psychological deformity, as such thoughts are detrimental to humanity.** A positive change in mindset is critical for, the time to save humanity is now.

SENT TO ANSWER A CALL THAT WASN'T MINE

In my father's desire to answer "Papa Ukochukwu"—meaning "Clergy's father"—he sent me to a Seminary school. I went, as I could not offer an opinion or dare to disobey my teacher father whom I loved so much, even though flogging was the main mode of correction I got, to the extent that I got flogged for ending an essay I wrote—when we were asked to write about our fathers—in primary five with this sentence, 'The only thing I don't like about my father is that, he likes to flog.'

My primary five teacher, Mr. Onuoha (AKA Garri ga agwu) could not contain his laughter after reading my essay and went to share this with my father, who was teaching in the same school at the time. My father summoned me when I returned from school with a cane in his hand; I knew I was in trouble. He then said to me, "I am going to flog you now because I enjoy flogging." I immediately realised what it was all about, but thought he was joking. He gave me six lashes of the cane and then warned: "Next time, before you write such a thing, you have to state the reasons why I flog."

It was such a harsh lesson to take but it gave me a clue on how to approach other things I wanted to raise with him, and in the end, I rendered my teacher father with many words speechless, following some interesting dialogue I had with him prior to his death. He became so shocked one day, after another encounter with him which revealed to me the immense power of the truth; I overheard him saying to my mother, "There's something about that son of yours ... something about that boy. Hmm, only heaven knows!" Though my father flogged like most teachers in his time, he loved all his children without reservation, and I couldn't have asked for a better father.

Anyway, I went to Seminary, and as young as I was then, I was looking out and listening for a call as the story of little Samuel was still on my mind. That call for my destiny to live a life of wearing collars never came.

It took me two years to confirm in my heart that I wasn't cut out for this but I was committed to carrying on because of my father. I was broken hearted the day I was called out from my class and told that one of my uncles came to take me home. I immediately knew my father, who was never ill, had passed on. I knew that for two reasons: 1) I had a disturbing dream and saw my father collapse trying to save our cat which was trapped in the garden. I was so disturbed by that dream I requested to go home, but due to the strictness of the institution, my request was declined; and 2) Never in history had my father sent anyone to go and get any of his children from school. My fears were confirmed when I saw my senior brother in the car.

The death of my father meant a quick exit from the Seminary school to everyone's disapproval and disappointment. I knew I had a different calling but was not sure what it was. In all, I learnt that one is never contented, happy, or free until they answer the call meant for them. I know I'm born to write because, as lazy as I can be, I'm overwhelmed with passion when inspired to write. In fact, I cannot stop writing. Prior to 27th November 2009, I had no interest in writing even an article. Since I found writing, I feel the sense of freedom and contentment.

The moral of this little insight into my life is: no matter who you are, do not get someone else to live your dream. Everyone's dream is different; therefore, if you can, simply provide an enabling environment where each child can identify and maximise their own unique potential. We are all born for a specific purpose and each of us, no matter how small or big, is vital to the overall equation.

I wish to inform my fellow tenants renting this world that, irrespective of how little or how much I know, I remain a student, studying at the 'University of Life.' I'm learning a great deal, but a bit disappointed when one of my lecturers told me that even the 'best' student would not be able to complete their programme and therefore, there will be no graduation for anyone in this university. In spite of my disappointment, I still find the lectures very exciting, as each day brings something new to shatter the assumption of knowing it all. This 'university' is not for the faint hearted!

I GREW UP THINKING I WAS A THIEF

It is not appropriate for a dog that sees itself as a pet to tell a dog that views itself as meat that it is behaving badly. As a child growing up in Africa, I was led to believe that I was a 'thief.' As one of eight children and two home helps, my teacher parents did not have the means to provide our needs, let alone our wants. Having three square meals a day was a luxury they could not afford on a regular basis. As a result, we ate at the appointed time, and everyone collected their food according to seniority.

If, for any reason, someone goes into the kitchen to take food when it was not the time for all to gather for a meal, they will be doing so at their own risk, because if they are caught, they would be treated like a thief. The treatment will certainly include flogging, humiliation, and possibly non-inclusion for that particular meal for 'stealing.'

As a lanky (always hungry) boy, food was all important and, on many occasions, I flouted the rules and got into trouble. It was not easy growing up as a boy in Africa generally, but particularly, in my household with two disciplinarian teachers. Even when someone else is responsible for taking food without permission, when no one takes responsibility for it, at times everyone gets the flogging because our father will assume that we are covering up for the 'thief.'

I got into so much trouble; I believed I was a thief. Having said that, I was still on the good side compared to my senior brother whom my father believed was the architect of everything that went wrong. Following my father's death, my mother depended on using some of my uncles to fill the gaps left by my father in terms of disciplining us. One day, a late uncle of ours, who was a Lawyer (Barrister Ben. Iwuala Ihenacho), came back from Jos, Plateau State, Nigeria where he lived with his family. My mother decided to go and report us for helping ourselves to the Stock Fish she bought for cooking soup. I was petrified, as I was expecting that my uncle would summon us as my father did for flogging—as I have been conditioned to expect to be flogged in those circumstances.

I overheard my uncle in his legal inquisitive way ask my mother, "What did you say again that you bought the fish for?" My mother replied, "I bought it in order to use it to prepare soup for them." My uncle then asked, "So you bought it for eating?" "Yes, Dede," my mother replied. Then my uncle said, "The children were eating it because you bought it for eating, as I believe they were hungry, so they are not thieving. When children are hungry, they need food and should be fed." As soon as I heard this, I quietly ran away in excitement feeling liberated and broke the news to my siblings. From that day, I loved that my uncle the more and remain his fan even in death. May your soul continue to rest in Peace, De Iwuala. You will continue to have a special place in my heart. This was a liberation he gave me without even knowing, and it gave me a new perspective on life.

Having gone through this as a child, my heart was broken when I learnt in November 2016 that a boy between the ages of 7 and 14 years of age was lynched in Lagos, Nigeria for 'stealing' food. My question is: How long would it take for humanity to wake up and save itself from itself? How long will we continue to live in a world of plenty and children are left to die as a result of malnutrition or lynched for eating because they are hungry? Even animals eat when they are hungry. Are we really sure we know what we are doing?

RECOMMENDATIONS FOR POSTERITY

In view of the importance and impact of leadership, be it spiritual or temporal, it is vitally important that anyone wishing to lead should subject or be subjected to a mental health assessment. Some would argue that the delusion seen in leadership usually commences after securing office. Though there may be some relative truth with such supposition, the fact remains that the disorder is not developed before, but intensifies at the assumption of office. The mental health assessors are vast in terms of the elements of the symptoms of mental illness. However, as it relates to leadership, the main areas of focus should be centred on the 'Five Finger' theory with particular emphasis laid on fixated interest on deluded concepts such as dominance, superiority, and inferiority linked to human beings as individuals, communities, and nations. This can easily be teased out because those suffering from these anomalies are often the last to know. The findings should be made public.

If the realities of our existence as human beings are based on a man and woman coming together for procreation, the tall needing the short and vice versa, a nation needing another and others to survive, and a particular religion having its identity based on the other/others and various differences for various purposes in individuals, cultures, and traditions, how irrational and insane are we, members of this one human race, that we are waging war on ourselves based on the same things that are there for our own good?

Those who planted the evil seed of dominance were wrong and ill, because to dominate is to destroy, and to destroy is to dominate. Anyone who agrees with the principles of dominance is irrational and ill too. Every finger is in its unsolicited position for a unique purpose meant for the good of the hand. Irrespective of size, no finger is superior or inferior to another, and none seeks to dominate another or others. Only rational human beings will understand this concept; the rest operate on jungle justice theories and concepts. Hence humanity is in dire crisis.

Think! Where is the mortal being who told you that your religion, culture, gender, ethnicity, colour, or nation is superior or inferior ... where are they that told you to dominate? Have you considered how sick they may have been? What is happening with your own brain, and aren't you able to think independently for yourself? Shouldn't those who are telling you and your children to go and destroy yourselves and fellow human beings lead the way with their children? And, when they provide proof that they have obtained their glory, then you can join in. Any finger that destroys another has, by implication, destroyed and weakened itself.

In this 'short' life we live as human beings renting the world as tenants, it is all about conviction. If you are convinced that you are standing on a solid ground and in the truth, the fact that you are misunderstood or entirely not understood does not mean you are wrong. It is on this unequivocal truth and premise I say that those individuals, communities, and nations that think dominance, superior, or inferior towards other unequal but equally important human beings are firmly in the wrong, because it is upon these weird concepts ... this deluded state of mind that extremism of all kinds are born and made manifest.

No individual, community or nation is more or less important than another or others, irrespective of size, because each is here for a peculiar and specific purpose and here to complement the other and the rest. As important as the job of a Prime Minister or President is, it is not more or less important than that of a cleaner, even though they are on two different pay scales. One is weakened without the other; we hold no value, no identity and will become stale without the other. I speak and write for no individual, community, country, or continent. I speak and write for humanity, one human race and one entity called the world we all inhabit for only a 'season.'

It just doesn't quite make sense! How can a visitor with no preconceived idea about anything ... a visitor with no idea about the womb or nation that would give birth to it ... a visitor that was so fragile and vulnerable suddenly assume authority and power to dictate to fellow visitors with different missions in a rented world, without consideration, regard, and respect? How and when did someone who arrived 'yesterday' so vulnerable become so important and powerful to dictate what happens to fellow visitors? What happened, what were the factors responsible, and at what point did these factors kick in?

Now, if dominance and violence are unacceptable in our homes, I don't, and can't, see how they can be acceptable, tolerated, or encouraged in any other sphere of human endeavours where each has a peculiar duty to perform, which deserves mutual respect, tolerance, and acceptance. Are human beings confused or what? Let it be known that anyone, past or present, with the ideology to dominate and with the mindset that associates superiority and inferiority with humanity, be it a religious, cultural, or political leader or follower, has psychological issues.

Think about it: if we are meant to eliminate any and everything different, there will be only us left. But then, can the hand function effectively with only one finger? Can an individual, community, or nation survive on their own? Can anyone prepare anything called food with one ingredient? How would the hand perform if the fingers seek to outdo and dominate one another, and would anyone recognise their religion if others did not exist? Think about this: if dominance, superiority and inferiority are not abnormal terms and concepts when associated with unequal but equally important human beings, why are people not bold in saying and/or practising them? Only abnormal minds do this, trust me. Humanity has a duty to deal with these cancerous concepts and those who believe in them!

If the realities of our existence as human beings are based on a man and woman coming together for procreation, the tall needing the short and vice versa, a nation needing another and others to survive, and a particular religion having its identity based on the other/others, and various differences for various purposes in individuals, cultures, and traditions, how irrational and insane are we, members of this one human race, that we are waging war on ourselves based on the same things that are there for our own good?

Those who planted the evil seed of dominance were wrong and ill, because to dominate is to destroy, and to destroy is to dominate. Anyone who agrees with the principles of dominance is irrational and ill too.

I will never trust, believe in, or worship any mortal being or immortal god who advocates dominance of one mortal being over another but will not be around to defend themselves. If such person or god cannot defend and protect themselves and want me to do defend them, how on earth are they able to protect me? If I have to defend and/or protect them, then they ought to be worshipping me, not the other way around.

As rational human beings, we need to appreciate that evil presents itself in liquid form with intense spreading ability. It is like the air we breathe with no demarcating lines, no boundaries, and can be blown to any direction. It is also like wildfire; once lit, it is difficult to control the pace at which it spreads or direction it travels. Evil, once around, can visit and can be visited, and there is no immunity from it as it is also self-destructive. The nature of evil is such that if it can happen somewhere in this world, it can happen anywhere within it. Evil feeds from practical, vocal, and silent sympathisers and supporters. Evil is never eradicated without uprooting it from its root.

Our world is littered with evil stemming from poor upbringing and socialisation, emotional poverty, selfishness, and greed based on the inferiority and superiority concept, poly - substance abuse, and with the added advancements in the production of hazardous technological gadgets at our disposal and passionate hatred of one another, we are in for a very rough ride in this world we have all visited as tenants. Which way, our world?

It takes a minute or even few seconds to drop a bomb, but it could take a lifetime to heal both the physical and psychological wounds caused by the bomb. The brain is superior to both the bomb and fist; after all, the brain is responsible for the bomb and instructs the fist. Why are human beings at the forefront of the demise of humanity, yet feeling civilised, rational and decent? Nothing occurs without reason, and improper thoughts bring about improper actions. The time to save humanity and save ourselves is now; tomorrow may be too late!

As individuals, we are all parts of the jigsaw puzzle that make up this one entity called the world, and no part of the jigsaw puzzle is without consequence. When we fail to do or say that which we are called to do or say, we stall and disrupt wheel and deny not only ourselves but humanity. In view of this, fight for, and retain, your sound ideals at all times, so long as they do not include sending your fellow tenant to go and wait for you in that common place you must attend. The common place shrouded with theories, as no one has been and come back to say exactly what is obtainable. What happens if, in the end, the 'enemy' you sent has a hold over you for eternity? Simply, hold firmly to your ideals but never lose sight of your present-day realities.

Mothers Why!

A father may build, but mothers (who are never absent at the birth of their babies, irrespective of how well or badly behaved), under 'normal' circumstances, are both primary and pivotal in the foundation-laying process of their children. This is because barring death, illness (mental or physical), and social upheaval, a mother is likely to spend more time with her baby during their formative years (0–5) more than anyone else. We all know how important foundations are to buildings, let alone a human being.

Why do some mothers recreate in their sons what they detest in their husbands or partners? "John, my son, your food is ready. John, my son, come and take your clothes; I have finished ironing them. John, please go downstairs; I want to tidy your room." The same mother will not see anything she had done wrong but is likely to become abusive to John's partner who dares not complain about "John, my perfect child."

If you are unmarried but intend to marry, please read "Cohabiting" inside the book entitled Humility of the Brain written in defence of humanity. Let's make things better for ourselves and our fellow tenants in this world we are all renting. Even a good father is a by-product of a brilliant mother somewhere along his lineage, as every human being is a product of the most powerful incubator (the womb). No matter how we want to mechanise life, no matter how crazy political correctness becomes, it is "mother earth, mother nature and mother nurture primarily for a reason" (Ihenacho 2014).

Our world has enough resources to go round, and the resources need not be shared equally, as all the fingers are not equal, and all the vehicles on the road do not consume the same amount of fuel. Our world also has enough space to accommodate twice the number of people inhabiting it, which currently stands at approximately 7 billion. Extreme greed and selfishness gripping many individuals and some nations has almost ruined our world. Is it possible that the mouth can eat alone and negate the need of other parts of the body? Where would the mouth be dwelling if other parts of the body die due to starvation?

Resist those who lie and say that the world is overpopulated or has not enough food to go round. This is the means they use to, if not justify, make the killing of their fellow human beings tolerable, and justify stealing and hoarding goods that may not be theirs. The truth is that nature, which is responsible granting each tenant residence in this world, is also responsible for granting other animals entry into this world. Looking at Britain where animals are protected and procreate without contraception, the country is not flooded with animals. Is this because other animals of different species are responsible for killing them or because their life spans are shorter? Well, in the animal kingdom, there will always be the strongest. Why have the strongest species of animals not engulfed Britain? Considering that these animals do not invent or produce food but depend on nature to supply their food, there is no shortage of food supply, let alone human beings who are not only fed by nature but can manufacture and produce foods

This is the moral lesson for us human beings. We need to be educated properly, not only academically but, more importantly, morally in order to fully comprehend and appreciate this. Without such education and insight, humanity will continue to wallow in severe ignorance amidst academic excellence and ingenuity. Remember, if you want to educate a person, choose a man, but if you want to educate a nation, then choose a woman.

Why are some people deluded to think that it benefits them when many are uneducated, immoral and acting stupid? We would still have people doing menial jobs if everyone is given the opportunity to be educated, especially morally, because not everyone will become a doctor and/or pass academic exams, but the ingenuities of humanity are numerous and mind boggling. Isn't this the same type of fear that gripped men which led to them preventing women from going to school and even casting a vote? Great Britain, for example, has not fallen apart; rather, has improved since women began to take their rightful place in society. In the same way, our world will improve and become better when every part of it becomes healthy and productive through the education and investment in world's best asset, the citizens of the world. How can the world, in the form of a human body, recover or even survive if it continues to instigate a war between the leg and the hand or think that it would continue to benefit and be immune from the dire consequences resulting from rendering the hand useless?

So it is advocated that for this lesson to be properly learnt, the girl child in particular who becomes the mother of tomorrow should be the vehicle of change. It is important to note that "no mother alive, no matter how well or badly behaved, has ever missed the birth of her baby, but there's always a reason or two why the 'best' father can miss the birth of his baby" (Ihenacho, 2014). This projects the vital link between the womb and the baby. As a result, on average, mothers spend more time with their children during their formative years (0–5) years barring death, physical and mental illness more than anyone else. Therefore, when mothers embrace 'the human fingers' theory and the need for every part of our human sphere to be healthy in order to secure a healthier world, they are likely to feed this to their children who, after all, are 'the future of our world.' Remember, "children only learn through observation; what they have not seen or heard simply does not exist" (Ihenacho, 2014). So, what do you think a child will be observing and learning from an academically and morally sound mother?

Keep in mind that the high, powerful, mighty; the good, bad, and ugly all hail from the womb of a woman and from a family of sort. It will be difficult for a child who understands and appreciates 'the human fingers' theory to negate the needs and importance of others whilst in government as an adult. Is it not absurd that in some parts of our world, women are barred from going to school, in spite of the fact that they lay the foundation for the future of our world—children? No wonder our world is severely under threat because the best and fastest way to brainwash children is to get their mothers to do the job, and the best and most effective way to brainwash women or anyone is to ensure they are not educated.

When I talk about education, I must highlight that moral education is even more important than academic education, because people with only academic education are like "beautiful places of worship with demons inside" (Ihenacho, 2010). They are usually those whose ideologies are based on 'me, myself and I,' and no one else. They are those who are willing to collect £7 million in bonuses whilst many in the same company are not able to provide three square meals to their children. The moral education based on 'five human fingers' should not only be taught in nurseries, schools, and colleges but should have its foundation in the families of this world. It needs to begin with parents and children.

When we talk about children, we talk about mothers first; when we talk about mothers, we talk about parenthood and families. Mothers are the live wire and coordinators of families. Women and men are different, just like the hand and leg, not equal but they are equally human beings, and none is more or less important than the other. The differences between men and women, especially in family situations need to be properly understood; else, the confusion, challenge, competition, and 'popularity' contest we are witnessing in families, against cooperation, partnership and collaboration needed between men and women will continue. As a rule, mothers under 'normal' circumstances, where death, illness, or social upheaval has not occurred, will spend more time with her babies during their formative (foundation laying) years more than anyone else. Fathers should play an active supporting role during this period.

The importance of foundation to even a building, let alone a baby, cannot be over-emphasised. Mothers also have to options of feeding their baby, whilst fathers have only one. It is not to be forgotten that there are exclusive nine months mothers generally have with their babies. Furthermore, the maternity of a baby is naturally never in doubt, but the paternity can be. Having said that, during teenage years, fathers come into their own, depending on the type of foundation laid primarily by mothers. At that stage, mothers play supporting role. If society denies women education (morally and academically), they deny children the same. If society negates the needs of the girl child, it automatically negates the needs of all the children that would come from that girl child's womb, which becomes counter-productive in the end to society. Is it not delusional to say that children are the future and negate the needs of those whose natural duty lies with laying the foundation for children?

Beyond that foundation, there is only so much a mother can do for a stubborn 12-year-old boy like me who pulled the trigger to my father's gun and blasted the mattress and wall at age 7. At age 12, I was strong and able to out-sprint my mother. I was lifting people up with my teeth and was entertaining people as a 'superman,' mimicking my late extended uncle 'Kill-we Nwachukwu.' I had started riding a motorbike, driving cars and was always on the go. My father was not always at home due to his many community engagements and other commitments. However, because my mother laid a good foundation which instilled fear and respect for my father, she was able to control me in my father's absence. When I did not want to do what she wanted me to do, she would simply, but firmly, say, "Ok, wait until your father comes home." I was wise enough then to appreciate what that meant. Those of us born in Nigeria will know what teachers of old, like my father, were capable of doing.

This is why I say the roles switch during teenage years with fathers leading the way and mothers supporting. Even a teenage daughter needs a strong father figure to guide and direct them. My parents were not perfect. Hence I am not, but they worked in partnership and always presented a united front. They understood that children are masters of 'divide and rule,' and will seek to play one parent against the other. The amount of work my father did with me between the ages of 12 and 14 when he departed this world contributed enormously to the person I am today, and I am most grateful. But it was also all thanks to my mother (though we didn't always agree) who laid a good foundation and kept me firmly on the ground in order to ensure that I never walked away from the great footprints my father left and imbibed in me before his invincible tenancy in this world expired.

What do you think would have happened to a stubborn 12-year-old like me if my mother led me to disrespect my father or have no regard for him during my formative years? I am glad that my three sisters have followed in my mother's footsteps and managed to produce some brilliant and inspiring children. This is because children more often than not replicate, minimize, or maximise behaviours in their homes as adults, which they observed from their parents during their upbringing.

These differences and roles of parents are only a guide, and not cast in stone. For single parents, many of whom do a great job with their children, there is no confusion as they are usually consistent with their approach. All children need is consistency, boundary, and structure in order to flourish. These differences in a couple's relationship are not, and should not be, a source of friction, but should be celebrated by both men and women.

The roles of mothers during formation years of their children are most essential and a virtue, not a burden, that must be appreciated by both parents and society at large. This is because even to have a good father means that a good mother planted a good seed somewhere along his lineage. For example, my boys cook because I cook, I can cook because my father cooked, and my father cooked because my grandmother defied a cultural norm preventing boys from entering the kitchen. This highlights the generational impact of a positive, singular and 'defiant' act by my grandmother! In recognition of how important girls are to our world, I have made a commitment to invest a percentage of the proceeds from the book Humility of the Brain to any organisation geared towards the education of girl child.

Families lie at the root of our world's crisis, because broken families lead to broken communities, and broken communities give rise to broken nations. Hence I know that the caption United Nation is an 'illusion' and only united in name, nothing else. This is because it is impossible to have United Nations when families of the world are broken.

There is no doubt that from the moment of creation or 'big bang,' leadership has been the domain of men. As a result, over 90% of our world is still run by men to date. Therefore, it will not be an exaggeration or unsafe to say that men are behind the mayhem we had seen and are witnessing in this world today, but in women lies the solution we desperately need. Read "Men are the problem, women are the solution" and see how the problem originated from a particular garden where a man named 'Adam' was placed in charge.

Once society empowers the girl child and all women academically and morally to adequately fulfil their vital roles, we may begin to see an end to our problem. These roles include the most vital role of laying the foundation which they are naturally primed to lay during the formative years of their children. Let it also be known that an academically and morally sound woman makes a better leader than a man of similar standing, because the female species are naturally equipped with not only the 'multi-tasking' gene but also the ability to distribute goods accordingly. Hence a hen with 12 chicks has no problem sharing food to all her chicks, no matter how small the food is.

Humanity must note that the weeds that appear in the farm uninvited to attack the planted crops and quickly outnumber them will never leave without the determined, deliberate and persistent action of the farmer to weed them out if the intention is to have a fruitful harvest. In the same way, those with the ideology of cheating, hate, and destruction are on the rampage with relentless determination to cheat, steal, kill, and destroy. They have little or no understanding that they are destroying themselves in the process. They, like the weeds, will never leave or stop without the concerted, determined, persistent and equally relentless action of each and every one of us if our intention is to have a better world. Humanity is therefore called upon to take a good look at the 'Abiding Legacy of the Man' and learn how to deal with our raw emotions in terms of our interactions with our fellow human beings. If humanity fails to heed these lessons, then there is a huge cost which can be seen in "The Cost of Inaction," all contained within the same book.

All hands need to be on the deck; it should, and must, not be left for the other person to attend to, because, as the Prime Minister of Great Britain, David Cameron, would say, "We are all in this together," and together we can do it; "Yes, we can," says President Obama of the United

States. Ladies and gentlemen, cometh the hour, cometh the man and/or woman!

Our Challenges are not here to destroy us if we are conscious of them; rather, they are here as opportunities for us to re-invent ourselves and win big for humanity. Only the insane would say that what we have now is working, because factually speaking, our world is spiralling out of control and unless we all join hands together to stop the decadence, we may ignore or neglect and rush ourselves into extinction or oblivion.

At the end of the day, it is all about parenting and upbringing at the end of the day. Those peers that put pressure, and those games and vile video makers are also products of parenting and upbringing. No child visits this world we are all renting with preconceived ideas, irrespective of their background. They only come with their diverse personalities but must make use of what they see and/or hear in order to develop them and create a brand of their own.

What a child has not seen or heard simply does not exist. Tooth fairies and imaginary friends will soon fizzle away, and all that will make sense to a child is what they saw and heard. At the base of whatever a child becomes in life (just like a house) is the foundation where parenting and upbringing reside. Giving birth to a long thing is usually the business of snakes. In this highly technological world with all manner of destructive gadgets at everyone's disposal, there need to be a basic, baseline parenting guideline for all would-be parents, bearing in mind that "Parents are like restaurant owners" (Ihenacho 2012), whose food is not just for own consumption but for the consumption of the wider public.

The baby one is carrying now will tomorrow become someone else's partner, colleague, neighbour or leader. And it is not just how well one's biological children are doing but how well-behaved other children are too, because your well-behaved children will remain at risk if your neighbour's children are unruly. Therefore, pay attention to that other child too and contribute meaningfully where possible and necessary to other children's wellbeing too. Every wrong thing said and/or done to a child represents a planted seed which can germinate and grow into anything. Therefore, consider not just how wrong but be driven by reflecting on the possible future impact and consequences if that seed is not uprooted at the earliest opportunity.

Essentially, the most critical part of the upbringing and parenting of any child is cohabiting and/or others involved in and around the child. The person one chooses to cohabit with is key to what is likely to happen to a child. In cohabiting, the uncooperative partner that says no gets their way, because in a game of two, the one who stops to play or scatters the game wins. As brilliant as any farmer is, the harvest will not be great if the farmer has a destroyer as a partner. The job of the destroyer is an offering of nature as no skill, education, or training is required to destroy. Irrespective of the best will and intention of one, if the other believes in 'your side, my side let us see who the children will side,' or believes that parenting is a popularity contest, competition, and challenge, the union will struggle to yield the right outcome. Hence one is as good as their weakest link.

Parenting living, working, and building together provides the right basis for children to succeed and is the best thing. However, with every good thing, it does not come easy. Those who expect it to be easy often destroy it. Every union, like a finger, is unique; therefore, a parent needs to beware of importing what they presume, based on stories, is happening in other people unions into their own. It is critical for those in marriage to note that it is highly unlikely for someone in their second or third-time marriage to say the latest marriage is worst compared to their previous evening if they regret not staying in their first one. It is also unlikely for someone single not to say they are happy, even though they are desperate to be in a union. When it comes to putting asunder, it is the role of the two people involved, because asunder are naturally out there. The self must not become dominant in a union of two. This is why it is important for each adult to be ready and be sure they are emotionally prepared for the me, myself and I to play second fiddle to we, ourselves and us. The destruction of our world routes to the destruction of families.

Cohabiting (who you live with), as I stated earlier, is key to what happens in the family and, of course, family is key to what happens in our world, because the leaders of this world, the terrorists of this world, the good, bad, and ugly routes from families of some sort. Everyone's foundation is laid in their particular family.

It is both important and necessary that every tenant of this world we are all renting understands and appreciates that one of the cancers confronting humanity is violence. Violence is a by-product of extreme greed and selfishness. Violence is often used by those who have little or no control over anger, fear, frustration, and temper which every human being goes through at one point or another. People who are violent are usually impatient, and as a result, they view violence as a 'fast track' to conflict resolution in their interest.

They use violence to intimidate, gain an unfair advantage or reassert authority threatened by sound reasoning. Violent people have no appreciation of the fact that violence makes a bad situation worse. Violence never reverses any wrong thing but destroys whatever is remaining. It may bring momentary peace but incalculable long-term crisis in the long run. Any 'peace' obtained through violence is a fake peace, because the victim is likely not to forget, even if they forgive. People who end up committing violent acts on a wide scale, including wars, gradually learn the acts of violence from their homes. Every human being can be violent. However, people who are brought up with sound ethics and with enough vocabularies end up discovering that the brain is more powerful than the fist. They appreciate that violence will not reverse the extramarital affair someone may have had or bring back a stolen good, but negotiations and discussions can improve things and possibly bring back stolen goods.

Violence would not only put the perpetrator in trouble but also could put both perpetrator and victim in harm's way, including loss of lives. No sound individual will see violence as a means of resolving conflict. No one should stand for violence, condone, support, or encourage it in any way, shape, or form. Parents, adults, and children need to learn to agree, disagree, or agree to disagree, following discussions. And when you agree to disagree, you must not return to the same issue unless there is new information to be explored. Ultimately, one must decide, following discussions, whether to forgive and carry on or say goodbye to a relationship. Under no circumstances is violence acceptable. It is critical to appreciate that self-defense is not violence, because the first rule in life is 'self-preservation.' However, self-defence has to be proportionate, not excessive, because it cannot be justified to kill a fly with a hammer.

In all, the key to peace nor harmony for humanity is the understanding and application of the word 'RESPECT' to both self and others. Anything that stops or hinders humanity from doing this is contrary to the working principles of humanity and will prove disastrous to humanity.

Finally, it is critical to know that any aspect of a culture, religion or tradition that is ill-informed especially, if they prescribe superiority and/or inferiority of one person or group over another can trigger psychotic illness and psychopathic and/or sociopathic tendencies. These should be avoided at all cost.

The Vision

Far away lay the most beautiful house which contains everything human beings need inside it—the peace, love, comfort, and security that humanity craves. Men are the pillars of that house, children the doorway into that house, but women hold the key into that doorway (Children) that would lead humanity into the peace and comfort longed for. Humanity needs to appreciate that the moral and academic education of the girl child and all women is key to open that doorway that leads to the 'promise land.' Human beings need to appreciate this quickly and take necessary steps to get into the safety and protection that beautiful house guarantees; otherwise, humanity will remain outside in the bitterly cold weather, high wind and/or temperature, and would likely implode.

Are we going to continue in the same vain and allow our chequered past to define our future, the future of our generation, and generations after us? Are women going to continue to blame men, and are 'black' people going to continue to blame 'white' people and vice versa instead of self-evaluating in order to identify and rectify their own contribution to the issues generating conflict? Is it that we do not know or have we forgotten that we need each other for our very existence and living? Are we going to continue this pattern and pass it over to our children to replicate with dire consequences? And, are we going to let the poorly laid foundations of our ancestors, who may be less intelligent and less exposed than us, dictate our future?

The hand of history is upon this generation, and without being an angel of doom and gloom, it might well be a matter of 'do or die,' bearing in mind that safety today has become an illusion to the sane mind. We can all recall that not too long ago, we happily booked holidays to Kenya, Egypt, Nigeria, and many other parts of our world with great joy and excitement, but today, we have to think long and hard for obvious reasons when seeking to do so.

Let me be clear; it can only get worse considering what is obtainable in "The Two Metaphoric Buildings Existing in Human Life" (Ihenacho 2014), where the first building containing human ingenuity has become a skyscraper littered with hazardous materials but the second building, which refers to 'human emotion' in terms of our social interactions, had remained at the foundation level and even decaying as we speak. The shocking part is the fact that it is this undeveloped second building that controls the first building, which has become a skyscraper. The collision between modern technological gadgets and poor/stagnated emotional development of human beings is providing the gravest of hazards to humanity. It is, however, hoped that human beings, being 'higher beings,' should have the capacity to cultivate high emotional intelligence in a similar way to their technological advancement. But this will take a lot of persistent nurturing to come through. When and if human beings get there, humanity can then claim to be rational. At the time being, our claim to being rational is merely based on assumption. But let it be known that our advancement in technology will prove harmful to humanity if we fail to advance in our interpersonal relationships as human beings.

How can humanity improve if people continue to sing the same plausible songs of political correctness that advocates positive discrimination, which is negative zoning and quota systems, not quality and best qualified and suited person for the right positions? What humanity wants is in total contrast to what it is prepared to do to achieve its desired outcome. In the same way, there are Christians, for example, who desire heaven but constantly pray, "Death will never see us in Jesus name"; some desire change but only want to keep repeating same old things that were responsible for the failure they are experiencing.

Let us pause, ponder, reflect, and project better for the posterity of our world. If this is what has become of humanity today, it frightens me to think of what will become of our children and grandchildren tomorrow if we continue to stand still while we spiral into total anarchy. Let's pull and work earnestly together for a better tomorrow. Those with feet must not depart without a footprint.

Three stage formula needs to be adopted in order to see positive change in humanity—and these are: the baseline, the differences, and the collaboration.

The baseline

Many have argued that the world would have been a better place if everyone stayed at their respective location without interfering with others. Some have also argued that the world would be a better place if everyone has the same language, culture, and tradition. Well, as plausible as it may sound, this would have been an awful position for humanity to find itself. Looking at the five fingers, one would notice that they all share a common base. This is the base that unites all of them, their similarities, and their common denominating factor.

As it relates to human beings, the common base is the one world they inherit and inhabit temporarily; the fact that they are all human beings, the singular blood that runs in each and the central colour of this blood for everyone is objectively red. On top of these is the standard similar route of entry unknown to each until they arrive initially without the concept of the womb or nation that bore them. The baseline for all also should have within it right to life, nutrition, good healthcare, education (morally and academically), and fulfilment of individual's potentials according to their respective abilities. But most importantly, the principles guiding the base should be founded on equality of unequal human beings, respect for all, appreciation, not just recognition of differences and equality in opportunity and before the law.

The differences

Again, looking at the five fingers, beyond the baseline comes the differences in all of them, as no two fingers are the same. These differences are of benefit to each finger and critically important for the usefulness and effectiveness of the hand. Though each finger is well contained and linked from the base, they are independently different in size, separate from each other and one another. These differences are necessary for exchange and cross-fertilisation of ideas, because if all the fingers were the same, the hand will either malfunction or would not function at all.

In the same way, beyond the similarities come the differences in each human being. Hence, no two persons are the same, even if they are twins, and each has peculiar attributes others do not have. However, irrespective of these differences, no one, none, irrespective of background, status, stature, creed, gender or nationality is more or less important than another or others, because each has a peculiar role to play differently from others. This is why the job of a cleaner is not more or less important than that of a prime minister or president, even though they are on different pay scales.

Each needs the other, and one cannot do without the other. The loss or malfunction of one finger causes the rest to over-compensate and forces the overall efficiency and effectiveness of the hand to weaken. In the same way, the loss of one individual takes a unique part out of humanity, which disadvantages the rest in ways unimaginable and incomprehensible. Everyone comes with their particular DNA, and once gone, cannot be replaced.

It is within these differences each has their unique identity and attributes as an individual, group, community, and nation; individual's dos and don'ts, different cultures, traditions, and religions. Looking at the five fingers, it is obvious that the hand can only be at its most effective when each finger is independent, strong and healthy and work in collaborative fashion with one another. This is the case with humanity too.

Only when each individual, community, and nation harnesses its unique attributes, becomes independent, strong and healthy and work collaboratively in partnership with one another will humanity be at its best. This is because no matter how independent any individual, community, or nation becomes, they cannot survive on their own. Hence, independence is an illusion, as human beings are interdependent on one another and each other.

Humanity is in crisis because it has from time immemorial gone against these principles by devising theories, concepts, and ideologies fit for the jungle—where some animals depend on eating others for their survival. Human beings are not wild animals. Human beings do not need to kill and eat themselves for their survival; rather, human beings are inventive, productive, reflective, projective, creative, and though being rational is not a given but an aspiration, human beings have all it takes to become rational by developing their emotional intelligence in the same way they have developed their academic and scientific intelligence.

As 'rational' human beings, what each needs to do is to individually strive to be the best we can be, assist others as individuals, communities, and nations to do the same where and when we can, because without that, we cannot be at our best. We lose nothing but gain immensely by doing so, because a candle loses nothing but gains by spreading more light from lighting other candles. We also need to learn to debate from our varying points of view with a view to agree, disagree, or agree to disagree. When we agree to disagree, we need not revisit the same issue unless there is new information to shed more light on the opposing points of view. Any attempt to impose or force an ideology, concept, or theory amounts to abuse, which creates bigger problem to humanity. Such usually stems from the deluded quest to dominate on the premise of superiority. Any acceptance of this deluded domineering drive stems from inferiority complex, and both are deadly to humanity.

It is a sign of psychological deformity to relate superiority, inferiority, and dominance to diversely gifted but equally important members of the one singular human race. You deprive yourself in the long-run by subduing another or others who have something unique and different to contribute. This is only one, singular human race with different individuals, religious groups, communities, and nations here not to compete but complement one another. The other races relate to dog race, horse race, and track race which human beings can partake. Being 'brown,' 'black,' 'yellow,' or 'white' does not take anyone outside the human race, so long as one can think, reflect, and project.

Red apples and green apples are still apples. White horses, brown, and black horses still remain horses. If human beings do not discriminate against horses, goats, and dogs based on their colours, is it rational they discriminate against themselves based on colour? It is one race, hence I love racists, and I am racist. Humanity should fall in love with being racist for it is one human race. However, being a racist as a member of the human race should not make one discriminate and not participate in a dog race and horse race, for we are all cohabitors of this one world we are renting for only a season.

When one, as an individual, community, or nation, thinks they are superior or inferior compared to anyone else based on whatever, they are simply ill and without insight. Because such thoughts are wrong, any actions stemming from them will be wrong too and disastrous to humanity. People with such thoughts need urgent help to correct their malfunctioning mind-set. All the evils of this world, from poor religious doctrines, dreadful political leadership decisions to terrorist acts (legalised or not), stem from these woeful and deluded concepts. Woeful concepts that have neither understanding nor appreciation of the fact that no individual, community, or nation is complete on their own or can go it alone and survive.

The Collaboration

In order to get things right, humanity needs to learn that no one, irrespective of background, should blame one without the other, because gullible society elects gullible leaders. There will never be a buyer without a seller. It is the inferior that gave rise to the superior, and the conquered made it possible for the conqueror. It is critical to understand that this malfunction is as a result of badly laid foundations by our ancestors. They laid this foundation on fear which stemmed from the fact they remained irrational as they did not know, let alone go through, the stages required of human beings before they can become rational.

The key to our development, posterity, and survival lies with all the tenants of this world. Each individual, community, and nation needs to commence the process of looking at themselves, healing, harnessing their peculiar attributes, and getting themselves right first. That is the foundation, and that will be followed by each needs exchanging and incorporating others through collaboration, compliment, and partnership in order for the beauty of humanity to shine through.

If, for example, one wants to look at slavery as an issue, they need to examine and understand the entire picture but ensure they fixate themselves with areas they contributed to slavery, because the seller is as guilty as the buyer. If it is to do with gender, remember, if you are a man, that you could never have an opinion or even be part of this world without a woman. If you are a woman, the same applies to you; you would not have been part of this world without a man playing a part. A son needs to look at his mother who is being abused by his father and say, "I will never do this to my wife," and a daughter should look at her father who is being abused and say, "I will not do this to my husband." It is not a competition, neither is it a contest or challenge; rather, it is complementary, partnership, and collaboration.

Pointing finger of blame will never help but hinder humanity. Sweeping negative things under the carpet is another way of asking them to keep repeating and commanding the children to replicate them. When each finger declares and proves its worth, the rest will have no option but to work in unison with reciprocal respect and appreciation. When one comes to the table empty handed, they are likely to leave empty handed or, at best, leave with leftovers. Don't expect to withdraw without depositing first. One weakens themselves, forces others to compensate, and weakens the overall efficiency of the rest when they fail to yield what is theirs to yield.

Never advocate and seek equality, because such is a concept that breeds confusion, as it is never obtainable. Men and women are different biologically, and no two persons are the same or equal. Men and women (just like the hand and leg) are not equal but different and equally important human beings. No two persons are equal, but everyone is equally a human being, just like the rest. The fight is not for equality but justice, respect, and full recognition, acceptance, and value each brings to the table. Just like the five fingers, no two persons are equal, but the inequality in size, status, or food consumption does not make any more or less important than the other. The concept of equality is fashionable, plausible but empty and without value, because it defies the vital ingredient for the growth of humanity which is differences. If fighting for justice and/or discrimination means holding the oppressor/s on a rebound, the aim is defeated, as everything remains the same from an opposing direction.

FINAL THOUGHTS & THINGS TO CONSIDER

Humanity needs to know the truth, shake off the shackles, and free itself for its posterity. It needs to realise that its foundations are wrong. Hence it is malfunctioning.

Humanity needs to realise that in all modesty, it is different and special compared to all others, including those ascribed as primates who are heavily favoured by nature. In the harsh wild, a three to four-year-old Ape is totally independent of its parents and can protect itself from all adversarial elements, but a human being in similar age group will simply be killed or die.

Apes and human beings and other animals may have come from one ancestral source, but they are on two parallel lines that have never met, and will never meet. Apes are born, live, and die as Apes, and humans being are born, live, and die as human beings. The similarities seen in all animals, especially in the reproductive process are clear indications that all animals came from the same source. The unequivocal differences seen when comparing other animals with human beings who are one of the weakest in physical strength, intelligence, and vulnerability in early years, offerings of nature, and nurture and what happens in later years point humanity to its original source.

The questions to ask are: How come nature favours and propels the life of all other animals but is primarily responsible for the sustenance of human life? Why is it that human beings are the only species that recognise, separate, and return to their parents in adulthood? How come human beings are the ones given the will to decide what they do...the will to reflect and project? How come human beings are the only species that can bring other animals, including Apes and Monkey for examination and study? Why is it that colours do not matter when it comes to other animals where colour is clearly relevant, and human beings do not discriminate against horses, goats, and dogs based on their colours but find colours difficult to manage in themselves? How come, for example, brown, white, and black horses remain all horses and capable of similar abilities, and they do not discriminate based on their colours from what we can see? But in human beings where such colours are not relevant (unless we want to continue to deceive and confuse ourselves in order to continue malfunctioning), we mistake colour differences and other differences critical for our survival and posterity for superiority and inferiority? Finally, why is it that children play along with one another without colours being an issue, but some adults struggle with colours?

Humanity needs to keep in mind that fear, pride, and stubbornness are the real threats confronting it but bravery and humility in seeking, knowing, and investing in the truth is the only way to save it. Knowing where one came from, where one is currently located ensures one's destination. Where there is confusion in where a journey began and confusion in the current location, then there will be confusion in locating the destination one intends. The truth can only frighten and make one uncomfortable if they are a liar. Those in the truth delight in the truth and are liberated. The truth is the only way. Shalom to HUMANITY!

ABOUT THE AUTHOR

Prince Ezem Ihenacho is Nigerian-born British naturalised man whose fascination about humanity knows no bounds. He is the author of Hard Hitting! The real truth about men, marriage & infidelity published in 2010, Your Child, My Child, Whose Child published in 2012, Humility of the Brain, In Defence of Humanity, published in 2014. He is the man behind the 'Five Finger' theory which is designed for the survival and posterity of humankind. He states that when this theory is understood, humanity will come to the realisation that the person who sold their birthright and the one who bought it are confused, wrong and equally guilty. This is because each finger is peculiar and unique. And though they are not equal, they are all equally fingers, as none can perform the role of the other effectively.

Prince Ihenacho is a father of five children, an ex-seminarian who aborted priesthood because he did feel he had the calling but believes he is called in a different way. He was brought up in one of the world's largest families. In his family, there is always up to sixty children growing up at every given stage. The blend of his childhood experience in his rural village, Amaegbu, Ekwerazu, Ogwa, Imo State, Nigeria and his adopted 'first world' country, England, has driven him to conclude that "wisdom, knowledge, and stupidity are not synonymous with any particular age/ age group, gender, status, nationality, creed, or ethnicity." Therefore, the ordinary, he states, can produce the extraordinary, and vice versa.

THE AUTHOR'S FUNERAL ORATION

I tolerated and was happy to tolerate false stories about me when I was alive but will have no stomach for them now I am dead. It is my intention to hold those who deem it necessary to give a false account of my stewardship whilst on earth responsible and hunt them down at any given opportunity. In order to ensure no one goes against my wishes and in line with 'advanced directives,' I decided to include this oration in this book, which is Driven By the Truth.

I took this decision because I did not want to be misrepresented in my absence in any way, shape, or form. I did not want people who never knew me to leave here today with the notion, "He was such a nice man who never had a bad word to say about anyone" or "He was a good and quiet man." I did not want any of these 'niceties,' because I know the real makeup of 'nice' and 'quiet' people in this day and age. Furthermore, it is the same accolade given to, if not everyone, most people when they are dead. I want none of that, because I am neither superior nor inferior to anyone but simply different. However, in that different lies the difference; else, all would be stale. I only saw the entire thing...the entire body called humanity, not parts of it, because as important as the hand is, it is useless on its own.

I came as a stranger with empty mind and weak body. Through no power of mine but others around me, I became aware and became strong. At one point, I thought I knew so much but later found that, the much I knew was still nothing other than a figment of my imagination in a world so big and mighty ... a strange world so full of mystery and wonder, and a world that welcomed me just 'yesterday' and today is bidding me farewell.

I was not as difficult or easy as I looked, and it is likely the same is applicable to you here present. I would easily have been a 'nice' person if I agreed that someone could do black magic and cause another person to commit murder. I would have been a nice person if I failed to say that someone's mental state relapsed because they were given an olive oil remedy in place of antipsychotic medication.

My silence would have obtained me the title of a peaceful man if I did not frown at the suggestion that the guilty can pursue a claim against innocent people for negligence, when it was obvious that those seeking redress were responsible for what went wrong. No one would have frowned if I agreed, without reservations, with political correctness, capitalism, religion, science and technology; indeed, if I agreed with that, the status quo has not gone mad. I leave with happiness that whilst I was here with you, I said all I believe needed to be said without fear or favour.

I did the best I believed I could, danced because I was given the feet, sang because I was given the voice, lifted people up with my teeth because I had a strong set of teeth, cracked jokes and was serious minded when I deemed it necessary. I had many flaws too, which confirmed my status as a human being sitting on a faulty foundation laid by the will of man.

I'd like to be remembered as an equal partaker in sin alongside everyone else except the 'holier than thou.' I attended places of worship because I was not a saint. Therefore, I never felt out of place, special or exclusive in the midst of fellow strugglers who were determined to try in our quest to be better tenants to this world we rent (and I rented) only for a season.

I was he that got into trouble many times for challenging, contesting, and fighting things many believed should be left alone. It could be those things that brought me here now, but I will lie in wait for the imminent arrival of those who played their part in what I have become this day. It goes without saying that if they did not do what they did, something or someone else would have still brought me here. It is a journey I knew had an exit. I depart in relative peace I don't expect many to appreciate or understand. I depart and await your arrival to that common place where everyone who visited and rented like me must attend.

I wish to tell all gathered here that any life without death is not a life, because death is a vital component and completion of life. Keeping death in mind as an integral part of the planning of life makes one not only humble but sane, but ignoring death whilst planning for life leads one to a life of recklessness and insanity. So, do not cry for me, but rejoice that I was here with you and hold onto those memories (good and bad), as they all have their respective purpose. I leave in the knowledge that the chain is broken, a part of the jigsaw puzzle is gone, and things would never be the same again, as I have left no duplicate of me with you.

A part of you has gone with me, and a part of me remains with you. But as we are each called home, that jigsaw and chain would be complete again. I am grateful for all my sorrows and joys whilst I was with you. In my joys, I was confused and ignorant, but in my sorrows, trials, and tribulations, I became wise, especially in knowing my true friends and those who genuinely cared. In all, I learnt that I wasn't such an easy or difficult person as I thought or as perceived by others, but my God knew and knows me best. Today, my absence from this world as we knew and know it is complete. I was old enough to know that my departure will make some sad and others happy. However, whether happy or sad, the important thing is for everyone to keep in mind that this departure is a must and a debt we all knew we owed. Therefore, where I am now is where you and everyone must be at one point or another. I have no more pain and leave you all in the peace of my Lord, Saviour and Redeemer, Jesus Christ.

Goodbye for now and see you all later, my dear friends. My journey is complete; my eyes which represented my physical being will start to decay with the rest of my physical body but my soul which represented my spiritual being has returned to our Creator and Maker, God Almighty! All I can say to all gathered here is; continue your individual journey with due care and attention for your respective exits await. Treat one another with respect; the same respect you deserve and crave, is what you owe to the other. Treat this temporary life as a race track. As individuals, communities, or nations, each should maintain their own track at all cost, because encroaching into other people's tracks causes friction that destabilises and creates a crisis. Be mindful! The person that means nothing to you, means so much to someone else.

I'd also like to be remembered as a sinner who continuously tried, an Igbo man, African, a Nigerian and a British who belonged to all nations of the world I visited and now leave behind. I (like you) was a full-fledged member of this one body with different parts for different purposes called the world, one entity, one human race and one human family. I leave in hope and faith that we will meet again but it would never be the same again.

Most importantly, I'd like to be remembered for insisting on four things whilst I was with you: 1) Irrespective of how well-behaved, your child remains at risk if your neighbour's child is unruly. 2) The greatest crime against humanity is the non-education (academically and morally) of the girl-child. 3) The only weapon known to 'man' is human beings, nothing else. 4) The ground upon which we, human beings perform our exploits including science and technology does not belong to any individual, community or nation.

And now, I take my final bow out of this transient world with these words: irrespective of what you think of yourself, what others think of you and which end of the spectrum you occupy in this world, if you are not aware of how incomplete you are on your own and how desperately in need of others you are then, you have a severe problem with your thought process and are in desperate need of help. Do seek help and you will find help. Peace be unto you all!

www.ingramcontent.com/pod-product-compliance
Lightning Source LLC
Chambersburg PA
CBHW030243030426
42336CB00009B/224
* 9 7 8 0 9 9 3 0 4 1 7 8 5 *